The
CAMDEN
TOWN
BOOK

First published in 2007
by Historical Publications Ltd
32 Ellington Street, London N7 8PL
(Tel: 020 7607 1628)

ISBN 978-1-905286-19-5
British Library Cataloguing-in-Publication Data
A catalogue record for this book is available from the British Library

Reproduction by Tintern Graphics
Printed in Zaragoza, Spain by Edelvives

The Illustrations
Illustrations are reproduced by kind permission of the following:

London Borough of Brent, P J Fahey Collection: *113*
London Borough of Camden *1, 8, 15, 20, 22, 23, 24, 29, 32, 33, 36, 44. 45, 51, 52, 53, 56, 65, 68, 70,
73, 75, 82, 84, 94, 96, 104, 105, 122, 131, 137, 138, 150, 151, 159, 160, 169, 170, 171, 172, 173, 174*
Roger Cline: *26*
Euan Duff: *83*
Miss M J Eiloart: *60*
Ettwein Bridges, architects: *85*
Alan Faulkner: *38*
Michael Goodall: *141, 142, 143*
Guildhall Library, London: *66*
International Distillers and Vintners: *92*
Richard Lansdown: *107*
Lawford's: *109, 110*
Leverton & Sons: *111*
Marine Ices: *118*
© Roger Mayne/National Portrait Gallery, London: *62*
National Portrait Gallery, London: *10*

*It has not been possible to track down the copyright owners of illustrations 35 (drawing by Heather Peri)
and 39 (by Hilda Bernstein). On application we shall be happy to make appropriate payments if
required.*
Other illustrations were supplied by the publisher

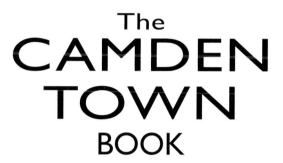

The
CAMDEN
TOWN
BOOK

John Richardson

HISTORICAL PUBLICATIONS

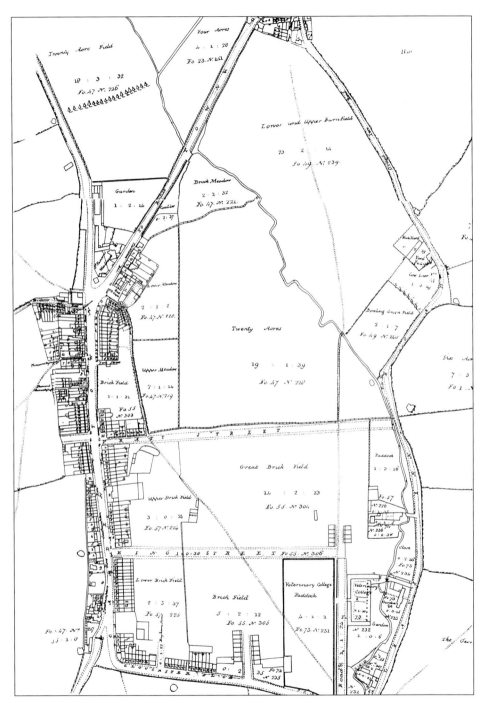

1. *Detail from Thompson's map of St Pancras parish, c.1800. Camden High Street is shown from the south at today's junction with Crowndale Road. To the north it branches north-west to become the later Chalk Farm Road, and to the north-east it becomes Kentish Town Road. Royal College Street is to the right, with the Veterinary College, established there in 1791. To the far right is the river Fleet and St Pancras Way.*

Introduction

By London standards, Camden Town is a new entity. The name dates from 1791 when the Camden family began to build on its land east of the High Street. The Southampton family had already begun a minor exploitation on the western side, but generally the area was fields, with the river Fleet crossing it on its way south to Blackfriars. Regent's Park was still to emerge from the farming land called Marylebone Fields. Cowkeepers were common, as were barns and the other structures associated with agriculture. A few buildings were worth the stroll from London, such as the Mother Red Cap for its tea gardens, but for a real walk and better views the energetic would have continued up the hill to Hampstead.

Camden Town developed mainly in the 1840s and 1850s, its desirability both enhanced and badly affected by the burgeoning railway lands north of the canal. Fine houses and jerry-built slums were erected in tandem and propinquity. But gradually almost the entire area deteriorated because of railway smoke, traffic and noise and this saw the conversion of innumerable properties into multi-occupation, thereby emphasising and adding to their inadequacies. It was not until the end of the steam era, and resurgence of urban living, that Camden Town recovered. And then came an unusual element. The disgraceful proposal in the 1960s to push a motorway through Camden Town created a blight which allowed entrepreneurs to form Camden Lock Market which, in its turn, was parent to many successors. Today, the Underground station, which once marked the division between everyday life to the south and the industrial area by and north of the Lock, now heralds an area of markets which people of a certain age will usually avoid but one that is full of bustle, music and desirable goods. The area's energy and growth have overwhelmed and vanquished the tidy ways of the local authority.

Just forty years ago it could not have been foreseen that in 2007 Camden Town would be one of the most popular of this country's tourist destinations. Nor would it have seemed possible that a person in a settled white-collar job would be too poorly paid to buy or rent one of the many terraced houses in the hinterland of the High Street and in Chalk Farm. Yet, for all the changes that have occurred, Camden Town is still very much like it was in the early 1960s – for the most part, workaday and shabby. There is a ferocious hunger for building land near the previously ignored canal, and some modern office blocks have appeared, alien to the old industrial buildings which survive. But, except that houses are in a better condition nowadays, the nature of Camden Town, outside of the market areas, hasn't altered a great deal. Its main street, south of the Underground station, is without charm or sophistication, still with the ugly fascias that chain stores and fast food joints prefer. It is not, as in Islington, full of bars, restaurants and estate agents which have displaced humdrum one-man businesses. In contrast, in Regent's Park Road there has been a distinct shopping revolution, where the old businesses have given up the fight against supermarkets, and have been superseded by niche shops selling to middle class people.

I have been particularly helped in compiling this book by the invaluable publications of the Camden History Society and the staff of Camden Local Studies & Archives Centre, especially there by Richard Knight, Mark Aston and Lesley Marshall. Jeremy Noble I have to thank for tracking down a photograph, owned by Miss M J Eiloart, of the twin villas that existed on the site of Cecil Sharp House - the only known image of those houses.

John Richardson

ABC Bakery

The Aerated Bread Company headquarters and factory in Camden Road was once a local landmark, just as its many restaurants were as familiar throughout London as branches of McDonalds are today. The site of its large building is now occupied by the Sainsbury supermarket.

The bakery's origins (and its name) lay in a mid 19th-century invention which avoided the use of yeast in bread making – despite its ancient use, rather frowned upon by temperance enthusiasts, and also by scientists concerned about hygiene. Instead, fizzy water to aerate and raise the bread was used in a process developed by John Dauglish.

The company developed through small bakeries, mainly in the City and its immediate northern hinterland, and by 1871 there were 88 establishments. From the 1860s they opened what one can loosely call dining-rooms as well which, of course, provided sure outlets for the ABC bakeries that supplied them. While most people remember Lyons restaurants, there were double the number of the slightly more down-market ABC cafés in Greater London in 1971.

The first ABC bakery in Camden Town, which supplied just local branches, was in Parkway, but in 1880 the company centralized its baking operations for the whole of London by building a factory at 21 Camden Road. Adjoining it were premises that contained **artists' studios**. In 1934 a new factory was built, taking in the site of the studios, designed by Sir Alexander Gibb & Partners.

ABC was acquired by the Canadian company, Allied

2. The ABC factory and offices at the corner of Camden Street and Camden Road, a site now taken by the Sainsbury super store.

Bakeries, in 1955. By then its Camden Town factory was a handicap, distant from the arterial roads that enabled distribution to a greater London and, as the company's London cafés were gradually closed, Camden Town's role in serving them diminished. The factory closed in 1982.

(For a fuller history see Robert Leon in *Camden History Review* 25, 2000).

Agar Town

William Agar, lawyer and King's Counsellor (1767-1838), lived at Elm Lodge, a three-storey, three-bay mansion south of today's Agar Grove and east of where the Regent's Canal crosses beneath St Pancras Way. Barker Drive in Elm Village approximately marks the site of the house, which was surrounded by mulberry trees. Agar acquired 70 acres of the Prebendal manor of St Pancras in 1810, an estate that extended from today's Agar Grove to King's Cross. He built Elm

Lodge soon afterwards for himself and his wife, a niece of the Earl of Shrewsbury, about the time that the Regent's Canal was being mooted (an Act was passed in 1812). Steve Denford in his study of Agar Town has noted that one of the proprietors of the canal company was the Hon. George Charles Agar, who would have been privy to the proposed route of the canal. Was he a relative of William and did he pass on this information to him? The implication here is that William took possession of the land knowing it to have commercial prospects, but at the same time he caused the canal company (and presumably his relative) great inconvenience and expense in fighting to have the canal diverted away from his house. He petitioned against the Bill in 1812 and later was granted an injunction against the canal company's surveyors entering his land. This led to a physical battle in 1815 between Agar's men and canal employees and compensation being awarded

3. *Elm Lodge to the east of St Pancras Way, Agar's home. This is depicted on* **King's Panorama,** *drawn in the early 19th century.*

4. *Counsellor William Agar.*

to Agar for this incident. It was not until 1818 that the matter was partially resolved.

Soon afterwards Agar sold his interest in the southern portion of the estate to the Imperial Gas Works – a remaining gas holder behind St Pancras station is a reminder of their presence – and two years after his death his widow Louise allowed building on the southern part of the estate, when houses with only 21-year building leases were erected. Inevitably, developers had little incentive to make much of them in so short a time and they were built with the minimum of facilities. Thus, Agar Town, north-east of Old St Pancras church, with Camley Street as it main artery, was brought into being.

King's Panorama notes that the houses were "four-roomed cottages ... built by Working Men at a ground rent, on the road side, payable weekly or monthly. The Leases terminate at the end of 21 years, which have brought together such a variety of Poor to the area

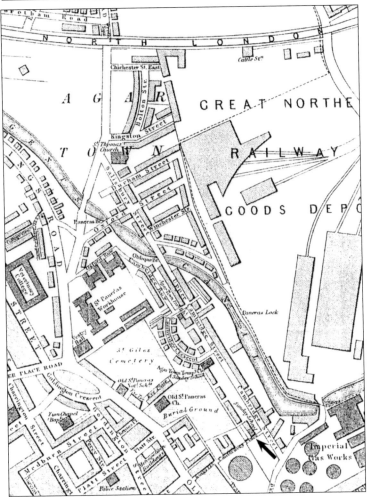

The area became synonymous with slum living though perhaps not so bad, as Steve Denford has shown, as contemporary writers claim. A contrast with its bad reputation can be found in an advert in *The Times*, no less, in 1847 from a laundress living in Agar Town, who solicits work from 2 or 3 families and boasts of a good drying ground.

Rapid change came with the railways, especially the Midland Railway into St Pancras, which gradually ate up most of Agar Town. Ironically, the once grand Elm Lodge on an 1863 map was completely surrounded by a Midland Railway coal yard.

We know little more of William Agar, but bizarrely his son's cricketing averages, while playing (two matches only) for Cambridge University c.1835, appear on the internet. (See Steven Denford, *Agar Town: The Life & Death of a Victorian 'Slum'* (Camden History Society, 1995).

Albany Street

When John Nash designed Regent's Park in the first twenty years of the 19th century, Albany Street (named after the Prince Regent's eldest brother, the spendthrift Duke of **York and Albany**), provided a strategic buffer between the wealth of the park villas and terraces, and the commercial and service area to the east. Much of the street has been rebuilt since the last war – on the west the Crown Estate has built flats and shops in the hinterland of the Outer Circle terraces, and on the east side St Pancras/Camden Council bought 32 acres from the Crown on which to develop the Regent's Park Estate, mostly

5. *Agar Town in 1862, sandwiched between the burial grounds of St Pancras and St Giles to the west, the railway goods yards to the east, and the North London line to the north. The Imperial Gas Works with their gasometers are to the south.*

known as Agar Town extending to the Gas Works... as to make it a Second Saint Giles, it being very hazardous for any respectable person to pass or repass without insult, or annoyance, as that locality received most of the refuse which the forming of New Oxford Street swept away". By 'refuse' the author means 'people'. An article in Charles Dickens's *Household Words*, written by W. Thomas in 1851, states that "the inhabitants exhibit a genu-

ine Irish apathy". He asserts that the roads are unmade, created between rows of houses opposite each other and churned into paste by carts from brickfields. There are no sewers – people throw everything out in front and there it stays; doors are blocked up with mud, and by heaps of ashes, oyster shells and decayed vegetables. Every garden has its nuisance: dung heaps, cinder heaps, whelk and winkle shells from costermongers."

*6. (Above) Albany Street c.1905 with Christ Church in the background and the old Ophthalmic Hospital on the right (see **Steam Power**).*

7. (Right) Christ Church in the 1940s.

designed by Frederick Gibberd.

Some much older buildings survive. The former Christ Church, at the corner of Redhill Street, was opened in 1837, designed by Sir James Pennethorne but later altered and decorated by William Butterfield. At about that time a stained glass window designed by Dante Gabriel Rossetti and made by William Morris was introduced. Rossetti's mother and sisters were members of the congregation here. The building is plain except for its graceful tower, and the massive doorway belies the relatively modest dimensions of the space inside. It was here that George Orwell's funeral service was held on 26

January, 1950, though he was buried in Oxfordshire.

The church was closed in 1989, its parish merging with that of St Mary Magdalene in Munster Square, but it is now the Greek Orthodox St George's Cathedral.

North of the church are the Regent's Park Barracks, built 1820/1 for the Life Guards and since then home to a variety of regiments. The present principal occupants are the Royal Logistic Corps of the 20th Transport Squadron. An 1831 guide noted that the barracks occupied an area of 8½ acres, and accommodated 400 men, horses, a riding school, infirmary and magazine.

South of the church the flats called Rothay cover the site of a former ophthalmic hospital, designed by Nash free of charge in 1818 and built for soldiers who had been infected with trachoma during the Egyptian campaigns of the Napoleonic wars. The two-storey building, opened in 1818, was emblazoned with the royal arms, and surmounted by a cupola. Patients were treated free, at one time by the surgeon and oculist-extraordinary to the Prince Regent. The hospital was not a success and closed in 1821, whereupon it became a detention centre for female prisoners while their new accommodation was being constructed at Millbank Prison. About 1824 the building was taken by Jacob Perkins who manufactured an innovative 'steam gun' and in 1826 it was occupied by Goldsworthy Gurney, an inventor of a steam road vehicle (*see* **Steam Power** *for these two gentlemen*). In 1835 the building became a distillery used to make Booth's gin and then from 1905 it was a bus depot. It was partially de-

8. *Albert Street, early 20th century.*

stroyed during the Second World War and the rest was taken down by Camden Council in 1967.

At the southern end of Albany Street is Melia's White House Hotel. This building was originally constructed as service flats in 1936, designed by Robert Atkinson. It was largely converted into hotel accommodation as from 1975 and then extensively refurbished in 2002 to provide 582 rooms.

Albert Street

Albert Street was developed about the time (1840) that Queen Victoria married Prince Albert – an occasion which promoted 'Albert' names all over London. (The northern section of the street was at first called Gloucester Street.) The building of this street on the Southampton estate coincided with renewed development on the other, eastern, side of the High Street as the Camden estate sought to attract well-to-do residents into villas off and on the Camden Road. It seems likely that there were simply not enough affluent people to make either scheme successful

in terms of social status. In a street directory fifty years later we find in Albert Street that it was probably 'respectable', but certainly not wealthy. There are signs of this in the presence of music teachers, dressmakers, and artists in stained glass.

However, built with more grandeur than most roads in the area, Albert Street was one of the first streets in Camden Town to be 'gentrified' in the later 1960s. Most houses are handsome, tall and conveniently placed, and they have attracted the professional classes with money to update them. Modern residents have included Julian Clary, Anne Diamond, Noel Gallagher and the actor, Denholm Elliott, who was at no. 75 and JD Bernal at no. 46 (blue plaque). **Peggy Duff** (1910-81) was at no. 11 (brown plaque); she was a St Pancras and Camden councillor and general secretary of the Campaign for Nuclear Disarmament in its heyday. Before that she held a similar post with the National Campaign for the Abolition of Capital Punishment, set up in 1955 after the execution of Ruth Ellis.

All Saints Greek Orthodox Cathedral

This church at the corner of Camden Street and Pratt Street is appropriately – given its later use – in Greek revival style. The architects were William Inwood and his son Henry, who also designed St Pancras New Church on Euston Road. Originally consecrated as Camden Chapel on 15 July 1824, the building cost £20,000, paid for by parishioners. Thirty years later it was still well patronized – 1650 attended on Sunday mornings and 1430 on Sunday evenings. However, numbers fell even before the last war and in 1948 it was taken over by the burgeoning Greek Cypriot community.

Anti-apartheid Movement

The Movement took up residence in Selous Street in 1983. This narrow road off Pratt Street when built was called Little Camden Street, but renamed in 1937 after the Victorian artist Henry Courtney Selous (1804-90), who lived for ten years in Bayham Street nearby and also at no. 28 Gloucester Avenue from the 1850s to the 1880s. Unfortunately for the local posterity of Selous, his nephew Frederick Courtney Selous (1851-1917) was an African colonialist, a colleague for a time of Cecil Rhodes (who, too, had local connections) and a famous big-game hunter. The Selous surname as an address was therefore an embarrassment to the Movement when it moved in and Camden Council agreed,

10. Henry Courtney Selous, a self portrait in oil, 1871. © National Portrait Gallery, London.

even though the street was named after the artist Selous, to it being renamed Mandela Street, commemorating the then still-imprisoned ANC leader. However, nos. 5-12 are still called Selous House. This piece of misplaced political correct-

9. All Saints church in Camden Street, early 19th century. The building was formerly the Camden Chapel, and is now a Greek Orthodox Cathedral.

ness is counterbalanced in Tanzania where the largest wildlife sanctuary in Africa, the Selous Game Reserve, shelters descendants of animals that Frederick Courtney Selous managed to miss with his rifle. The Anti-Apartheid Movement in this country was wound up in 1994 after the freeing of Mandela and the first democratic elections in South Africa.

Arlington House

Arlington House at the northern end of Arlington Road was originally a Rowton House, one of a small chain of London hostels for men. They were not the 'homeless hostels' of modern times, although certainly homeless men could stay, but they were also used by itinerant men working in London for a set amount of time. They were a great contrast to the common lodging houses of the day, which were one of London's scandals.

The hostels were founded by Montagu William Lowry-Corry (1838-1903), the first and last Baron Rowton, who had been Disraeli's private secretary. His sympathy for men who needed respectable hostel accommodation began when he was involved with the Guinness Trust, a charity formed to provide artisan housing. What Rowton wanted was to build a very large hostel with comfortable beds, proper sanitary arrangements, and good food at prices that such men could afford. The prospects were not good – if the venture failed the building would probably be of no use for any other purpose.

Rowton put up his own money to begin. His first hostel was opened at Vauxhall in 1891, little more than a year after he first proposed it. The aim

11. The first and last Baron Rowton.

was for it to be a working-man's *hotel* rather than a respectable doss-house, and he expected the inmates to treat the facilities with respect and discipline. Each lodger had a private cubicle, a locker and his own window – they were small cubicles, hence when you look at Arlington House you will see a great many narrow windows to match the 5' wide cubicles. Religion was not thrust upon the inmates.

The second Rowton House (1896) was near Mount Pleasant on a site now occupied by an ugly Holiday Inn. In Camden Town, the largest of the Rowton Houses, designed by H B Measures, was opened in 1905; it had 1103 beds.

After the last war conditions at Arlington House worsened and as property values in the area went up, so the hostel for homeless men appeared to be a blight on the area. Old-style disciplinary rules still existed, summed up in a punishment book for the early 1980s in which, for example, inmates were fined, usually £7, for bed wetting or other misdemeanours.

In the 1980s the building was taken over by the Greater London Council, and later went to Camden Council. Today it is administered by a housing association called Novas Ouvertures.

Artists' studios

The **Camden Town Group** is Camden Town's most famous niche in visual arts history, but there have also been at least four sets of artists' studios in the area. The least known, and the oldest, was on the site of the present **Sainsbury** supermarket in Camden Road. The 1895 street directory lists six artists, none of whom went on to fame. The same may be said of the artists in the Camden Street studios listed in the same directory, although Henry Bursill, a sculptor who modelled the figures for Holborn Viaduct, was an early resident, as were Andrea Lucchesi and Alfred Southwick, both sculptors. In the 1920s Stanley Wood, magazine illustrator and specialist in equestrian painting, worked there.

These studios were built 1865-9 by William Roberts. They consisted of nine single-storey buildings in two rows facing each other. They fell victim to the St Pancras Council zest for clearance schemes in the 1960s, but at least in the redevelopment of the area seven new studios were built, together with an inadequate exhibition hall which hardly functioned as such and was eventually used as a community room. The Hungarian émigré sculptor Peter Peri (1899-1967) was the last artist of note to have a studio there. Coincidentally, Peri's work, mainly small figurative sculptures, was shown in 2003 at

12. *Primrose Hill Studios, 2007.*

13. *Residents of Camden Studios in Camden Street in 1892 (left) and in 1922.*

14. *Henry Wood, resident of Primrose Hill Studios.*

Camden Studios.	Camden Studios.
3 Lucchesi Andrea C., sculptor	1 & 2 Lucchesi Audreas C., sculptor
4 Clifford Edwd.C.,artist	3 Cardon Claude, artist
5 James Gilbert, artist	4 Dimelow Miss, artist
6 Sime Sidney H., artist	5 Smith Phil, artist
7 De Botwor Charles H. B., artist	6 Rowe Grant, artist
8 Taylor Tom, artist	7 Cooper J. A., artist
9 Wood Stanley, artist	8 Southwick Alfred, sculptor
	9 Thomas H., sculptor

Leeds City Art Gallery together with that of Ghisha Koenig, who also made small metal sculptures, particularly of people working in factories. Koenig (1921-1993) had a studio in Cliff Road Studios, built by George Wolton 1968-72; her studio there had been previously occupied by the constructivist sculptor Naum Gabo (1890-1977).

The twelve Primrose Hill Studios still exist, concealed behind Fitzroy Road in Chalk Farm, grouped in cottage style around an interior courtyard. They were the work of a local builder, Alfred Healey, and were built between 1870 and 1882. An unusual feature was that the studios were provided with a lodge in which lived a keeper and his wife who supervised the buildings and the cleaning, and even provided meals. This arrangement continued until the 1940s and was described in Joseph Hutton's *By order of the Czar* as similar to that of an old-fashioned college or lawyers' Inn.

The most notable artist/resident was Arthur Rackham (1867-1939), the celebrated illustrator of children's books. Other artists there have included Patrick Caulfield (1936-2005), John William Waterhouse (1849-1917) at nos. 3 and 6, and Collier Smithers (1867-1943) at no. 5. Residents are not necessarily visual artists. The conductor, Sir Henry Wood (1869-1944) and the actress Martita Hunt (1900-69) also lived in this cosy enclave.

Baths and Washhouses

The first public baths and washhouses in Camden Town were built on a piece of waste land in Plender Street, just east of the Parr's Head pub. These opened in 1868 against the opposition of those who habitually fought any measure which would increase rate expenditure. The building was popular. Within a year 145,000 had used the baths, and there was a frequent use of the laundry facilities. It was noted that the women coming to do the family washing stayed an average of 3½ hours, washing, man-

15. *The Savoy Turkish Bath in Kentish Town Road, near Camden Town Underground station.*

gling, drying and ironing, spending an average of 5½d.

These baths were demolished when the present housing development occurred. Appropriately, a launderette stands on part of the site.

More exotically, the Camden Town Turkish Baths opened in 1878 at 11a Kentish Town Road, just north of Camden Town Underground station. These closed *c*.1916, when they were known as the Savoy Turkish Baths.

Bayham Street

The street derives its name from Bayham Abbey in Kent, one of the Camden family properties.

The northern section was built in the early 19th century, but the southern stretch was developed as from the 1840s.

On the site of no 141 was the home of the penurious **Charles Dickens** family and at nos. 85-93 the **Dalziel brothers** established their famous engraving and printing works in the 19th century. The **St Martin's Almshouses** were built in 1817. At nos. 116-134 is the former factory of Ernest F. Moy & Co., founded in Pratt Mews in 1895 by three local men, Messrs Moy, Bastie and Fox – a descendant, Harold Bastie, was mayor of St Pancras in the 1960s. According to Camden History Society's *Streets of Camden Town*, the

firm was principally concerned with the application of electricity to photography. In 1900 they produced a cine-camera – it was one of these that accompanied Captain Scott on his ill-fated 1905 Antarctic expedition. It is possible, claims a website, that a Moy camera shot the first Hollywood film. Certainly Moy cameras were standard pieces of equipment in many film studios. The firm continues in Boreham Wood where the famous 'Elstree' studios are located, trading as Scubacam, making underwater film and video equipment.

Bedford New Town

A name which has fallen into disuse for the area south of Crowndale Road, stretching from Hampstead Road to Pancras Road and touching the fringes of Euston Station. Originally a tract of farmland called Fig's Mead, it was owned by the Dukes of Bedford and names such as Hurdwick Place, Ampthill Square, Harrington Square, Oakley Square, Lidlington Place and Goldington Crescent reflect those of the Dukes' country estates. Development began in the 1830s, but within a decade the **London & North-Western Railway** intruded, slicing its way through the western part of the estate on its way to Euston. None of the three 'squares' was remotely square, and Ampthill survives today only as a name for a housing estate. The three tower blocks that form part of the estate, named hopefully after Lakeland features, have an interesting story. The area was damaged by bombing during the last war and plans were made in the 1950s to build tower blocks, then thought to be the answer to virtually every need in public housing. It did, however, take many years for the land to be acquired and it was not until the late 1960s that development could begin. By then the designs for the blocks, formulated much earlier, were hopelessly outdated and though modifications were attempted to make them less like a Moscow suburb, they were still unacceptable and the blocks were reclad in the 1980s to make them look more inviting. Some of the Camden councillors on the planning committee of the late 1960s wanted to drop the scheme altogether and

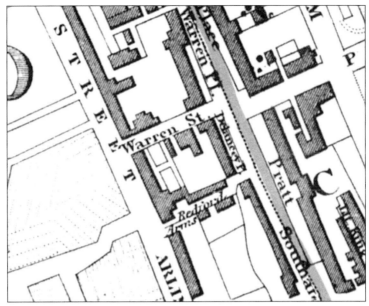

16. The Bedford Arms in Arlington Street, and its premises in the alley between it and the High Street. From an 1834 map.

start from scratch on the site, but were advised that they would be personally surcharged for the costs of such a cancellation and the compensation to the architects.

Most of Bedford New Town is now housing estate, though one side of Oakley Square survived the council blitz of c.1965. St Matthew's church, on the site of today's St Matthew's Court, adorned the elongated oval garden in the middle of Oakley Square. This was built 1852-6, designed by John Johnson, but pulled down in 1977.

Bedford Tavern and Music Hall

The Bedford Arms Tavern was at 80 Arlington Road, by the alleyway called Mary Terrace. It had grounds attached between Arlington Road and Camden High Street and these were turned into a small pleasure garden, respectable at first, where people came for tea and to be entertained in the Long Room. Balloon ascents are noted in 1824 and 1825, the latter conveying two women as well as the aeronaut. A music hall was built in the grounds

17. Mr Graham, an experienced balloonist took Mrs Graham for a trip into the 'aerial regions' in June 1825 from the Bedford Arms. A Mrs Forbes accompanied them.

15

18. *A Sickert depiction of the music hall at the Bedford.*

some shops on Camden High Street had been bought it was possible to give the new theatre a main road frontage – previously the main entry was from Arlington Road. The purchaser of the shops, B P Lucas, together with Ted Johnson, demolished the old hall (closed on 9 July 1898), and opened a new theatre, at first called the New Bedford Music Hall, on 6 February 1899. This was to become the **Bedford Theatre** (*see below*).

(For a more detailed account see Marion Kamlish, *Camden History Review* 19, 1995).

in 1861, a development by R C Thornton. It was this theatre that cast such a spell on the artist **Walter Sickert**, whose many drawings and paintings of the place have brought the old Bedford an exceptional posterity. The *Camden & Kentish Town Gazette* of 1870 commented: "When some eight years ago it first sprang into existence it was nothing better than a long, ugly room badly lighted and badly ventilated, penny-gaffy in its appearance, and most decidedly penny-gaffy as regards the nature of its entertainments. It did not however, long continue in this condition, for soon it took upon itself a gallery, which originally stretched solely across its lower end, but which ultimately (1864) came to be extended along its two sides."

In 1867 the hall was taken over by Edward Weston, an entertainment entrepreneur. He had been the proprietor of what became the Holborn Empire, and also The Retreat, a pleasure garden to the west of Highgate Road, on a site later covered by Midland Railway

yards. For a short time he called his new theatre in Camden Town the Royal Maison Dorée, but within a year he reverted to the Bedford, which the local press sniffily said would remind respectable inhabitants of Camden Town of the hall's "questionable notoriety". Weston went bankrupt the same year to the tune of £27,000.

It is often asserted that this theatre burned down, but Marion Kamlish has discovered this was not the case. Once

Bedford Theatre

This theatre replaced the old **Bedford Music Hall**, and opened on 6 February 1899. It remained a music hall for much of its existence until the mid-1930s. The architect was Bertie Crewe, and the audience capacity was 1168. The well-known names of music hall appeared here – Marie Lloyd, Vesta Tilley, George Leybourne, Gracie Fields, Chaplin – and also Trottie True, whose career was made famous in the Jean Kent film of that name in 1949, which was set in the Bedford. The

19. *The Bedford Theatre c.1905.*

20. An Edwardian Bedford Theatre programme.

comedian, Jimmy Nervo, made his first appearance on the stage here in 1909, aged 12.

The Bedford became, like so many theatres, a cinema from 1933 to 1939. After the war the Bedford was in a bad way. Repertory was tried in 1947 and variety was embraced in 1948. Drama was revived when Donald Wolfit took on its direction with productions of Shakespeare, and then Pat Nye took on the lease with a production of *Lady Audley's Secret*, which starred the film actress Anne Crawford. On first night George Robey arrived by stage coach, and in the audience were Laurence Olivier, Jean Simmons, Glynis Johns and Bransby Williams. Oddly, the theatre produced in 1950 the first play of Peter Wildeblood about the failure of the government's groundnut scheme in Africa. The Bedford closed in January 1951.

The building stood derelict for many years. The Labour Party members of St Pancras council proposed to use its site to build a central library for the old borough, but upon losing control of the council to the Conservatives in 1959, this plan was abandoned and instead the central library was built on Euston Road together with the Shaw Theatre.

What was left of the Bedford was demolished by 1969 and the site has been redeveloped since.

The Bedford is associated with the famous trial of Henry Hawley Crippen who murdered his actress wife, **Belle Elmore**, at their home in Hilldrop Crescent, Islington on about 31 January 1910. Elmore was an undistinguished music hall artist who often appeared at the Bedford. In January 1907 she made her last appearance there, singing *Down Lovers' Walk* and what was known as a 'coon' song. That week there was a strike by music hall artistes for higher wages.

21. *The Bedford Theatre awaiting demolition.*

BEDFORD THEATRE

CAMDEN TOWN   EUSton 3047

Licensed by the Lord Chamberlain to   ...   .   PAT NYE

TUESDAY, JAN. 24th   FOR TWO WEEKS

"THE SHAUGHRAUN"

By DION BOUCICAULT

CAPTAIN MOLINEUX   ...   DIRK BOGARDE
(a Young English Officer commanding a detachment at Ballyragget)
(By permission of the J. Arthur Rank Organisation)
ROBERT FFOLLIOTT ...   RICHARD LONGMAN
(a Young Irish Gentleman, under sentence as a Fenian—in love with Arte O'Neale)
FATHER DOLAN...   ...   .   JOHN KELLY
(the Parish Priest of Suil-a-beg—his tutor and guardian)
CORRY KINCHELA *(a Squireen)*   ...   TONY QUINN
HARVEY DUFF ...   .   LARRY BURNS
(a Police Agent in the disguise of a peasant under the name of Keach)
CONN   ...   .   BILL SHINE

22. *The cast list for this Boucicault play in 1950 included Dirk Bogarde.*

Elmore crossed the picket line at the Bedford, which included Marie Lloyd, who remarked that it would be best to let her through as she would soon empty the house anyway.

Alan Bennett

The writer Alan Bennett's long residence in Gloucester Crescent was partly explored in his story *The Lady in the Van*. Bennett (b.1934) befriended a Miss Shepherd (d.1989), whose clapped-out Bedford van was habitually parked in the Crescent and increasingly at the mercy of parking restrictions. The playwright allowed her to park temporarily on his own driveway free of charge – and there she stayed for 15 years. She was, recorded Bennett, a trained concert pianist, an ex-nun, and a "bigoted, blinkered, cantankerous, devious, unfor-giving, self-centred, rank, rude, car-mad cow." Their long relationship, originally published in print, was made into a highly successful play which opened in 1999, starring Maggie Smith as Miss Shepherd.

23. *Bowmans' store c.1905.*

Bennett, who is very fond of Camden Town, made head-lines in 2006 when the Regent Bookshop in Parkway closed. This prompted him to urge the public to boycott large chain bookshops which drove small concerns such as the Regent out of business.

Bowmans

Bowmans was once the largest store in Camden Town. At its most extensive in the 1960s it occupied 112-138 High Street, selling mostly furniture, but also other household goods. Early expansion relied on sales of mahogany furniture, but after the last war pine was king. The firm began as upholsterers at no. 108 in 1864, run by the Bowman brothers, Thomas and Robert, sons of a Lakeland farmer. Gradually the shop was extended to Greenland Street, but a fire in 1893 was a fortunate occurrence for it allowed the rebuilding of the store in arts-and-crafts style – see the motifs surviving on the fascia of the red-brick part of the building. The family still had an interest in the business until 1971, when Jack Bowman,

19

24. *A Bowman room setting in the early 1960s.*

grandson of Thomas, retired.

Bowman's was then absorbed into a group of stores which included the famous Gamage's in Holborn. In 1974, when the latter were building a new store in the West End, they moved temporarily into part of the Bowmans building, but left in 1979. The vacant part of the building was then left unoccupied and the whole store had its closing down sale in April 1982. The non red-brick part was then demolished and redeveloped.

25. *The premises of the Boys' Home in Regent's Park Road.*

26. *Stacking wood at the Boys' Home, c.1900. From a booklet entitled* The Story of the Boys' Home.

Boys' Home, Regent's Park Road

The Home for the Maintenance by their own Labour of Destitute Boys not Convicted of Crime was established in 1858 as an industrial school at 44 Euston Road by two gentlemen who, though unrelated, both had the name of George Bell. When the Midland Railway came to Euston Road to build St Pancras station, the Home was removed in 1865 to the corner of Regent's Park Road and King Henry's Road, where it occupied some unfinished premises on the Eton College estate. Here it remained until 1920. One of the Bells, George William, was secretary of the Soldiers' Daughters' Home in Hampstead, which his sister, Leonora, supervised.

The routine for the boys was strict by modern standards. They rose at 5.45am, had drill at 6.15, then cleaned the premises, after which they had breakfast at 7.45, followed by prayers and work until lunch. There were lessons in the afternoon, wood-chopping at 5pm, then more prayers and play until bedtime at 8.30.

Eventually the Home took up space in adjacent houses, with enough room – rare for such institutions – for each boy to have his own bed. The boys were taught carpentry, printing, tailoring and music, apart from the usual school subjects. Gillian Gear, in her article on the school *(see below)* notes that a number of boys were of sufficient skill to go on to work at the William Morris Company to make furniture. A rocking horse made by the boys is now held by the Bethnal Green Museum of Childhood. By 1911 it was reported that the Home had 34 boys from the age of seven upwards.

Over the years the Home helped over 1,000 boys with a mixture of good education and encouragement to learn skills. (See Gillian Gear, *Camden History Review* 18, 1994)

The Brecknock Arms

Now known as the Unicorn, the Brecknock Arms, at the corner of Brecknock Road and Camden Road, was the scene of a famous duel in 1843. At that time, though the new road from Camden Town to Holloway had been laid out, not much had been built upon

27. *The Brecknock Arms Tavern in Camden Road in 1856. It was then run by F. Butcher, who also provided livery and bait stables.*

– the first villas in nearby Camden Square were just being constructed. The Brecknock (named after the place in Wales in which Elizabeth, Earl Camden's wife, was born) was then still a country retreat with the obligatory tea garden, sports ground and bowling green. An advertisement survives for a grand 'pedestrian' event when a celebrated walker was backed to walk 1750 miles in 1000 hours on a measured circuit in the grounds.

The Brecknock was still an isolated building meriting a country walk, but it achieved notoriety in 1843 when two men, Lt Col Fawcett and his brother-in-law, Lt Munro, fought a duel with guns in the grounds of the inn. Neither was killed at the scene, but Fawcett was shot. The owner of the Brecknock was away, his wife was ill and a waiter refused to accept the wounded man in to the premises and Fawcett was

instead taken to the Camden Arms in Randolph Street for treatment. However, he died next day.

An inquest was held by the famous Thomas Wakley, founder of *The Lancet* journal, his jury consisting of 14 local residents. It seems that the dispute arose from an argument the two men had had over the handling of Fawcett's affairs by his brother-in-law while the former was abroad on army business. The next day Munro sent a second around to Fawcett to issue a challenge.

The duel provoked a great deal of public comment, for there was a general feeling that duellists, who were almost always from the wealthier classes, were allowed to get away with murder – this had applied particularly to Castlereagh, Wellington and Cardigan. In the same year the Anti-Duelling Association was formed to get rid of a practice

that was "sinful, irrational and contrary to the laws of God and man".

In the event one of the seconds and the surgeon who attended the Brecknock duel were put on trial for assisting the contest. Both were found not guilty. In the meantime Munro disappeared to the continent, and he was not brought to trial until 1847. He was found guilty, but escaped execution and received just one year's imprisonment.

Britannia Hotel

This stood at the southern corner of Parkway and Camden High Street. It first appeared in the licensing records in 1777, and closed in 1962, though above the old premises there is still a figure of Britannia. The ground floor has been entirely rebuilt and is used by shops.

28. *The Britannia Hotel at the corner of Parkway and Camden High Street, probably in the 1850s. The statue of Britannia is still on the present building, though the ground floor is now considerably altered.*

Brown's dairy

The dairy was a renowned feature of Camden Town, occupying a prime position at the apex of Camden High Street and Kentish Town Road, where the bank building now stands in front of the Underground station. It was known as the 'Cows' cathedral', probably from its pinnacled exterior. The illustration here has the words 'Established 1790' emblazoned, but if so it wasn't here – the St Pancras map of *c*.1800 has the second St Pancras **workhouse** on the site. Mr Brown probably began business on this site in the early 1820s.

Brown kept cattle in the fields behind the premises and was one of many cowkeepers in the parish. In 1857 a comprehensive report claimed that some cowhouses were almost underground and that 20 had inhabited rooms above them. The aim of some cowkeepers was to keep the animals as warm as possible as this favoured the formation of cream. Disease was rampant and one cowkeeper, who kept between 400 and 500 cows, lost two cows a week from sickness. Furthermore, much milk was tainted with disease. The St Pancras Medical Officer of Health was keen to see all

29. *Brown's Dairy at the junction of Camden High Street and Kentish Town Road. The site is now occupied by a bank and the Underground station.*

30. *William Bruges with St George. From William Bruges's Book (British Library MS Stowe 594.f.5v)*

sticks kept in this chapel to the church he was rebuilding in Stamford. In the Cantelowes court rolls (which cover the Camden lands to the east of the High Street) his landholdings are recorded but, tantalizingly, without hard evidence of the precise location of his house.

Bruges appears in state records as having entertained the Holy Roman Emperor Sigismund during his visit to this country in 1416, a year after Bruges' appointment as Garter King. Sigismund was not a man to be trifled with, having seized power in a disputed election, and having burnt the Czech religious reformer Jan Hus at the stake in 1415. Bruges must therefore have had some trepidation about entertaining his guest in an appropriate manner in remote Kentish Town..

Bruges met the Emperor's procession, which had come from Ely Palace in Holborn, probably at today's King's Cross. The assembly was of great magnificence. It consisted of representatives of the livery companies of London, together with the Lord Mayor and aldermen, the king's trumpeters, officers at arms, esquires and knights, the Bishop of Ely, the Dukes of Briga and Holland, the Prince of Hungary and other court luminaries. Bruges knelt bareheaded to receive them and then escorted them to his house for entertainment and feasting. Minstrels and sackbutts diverted them and then the food, which included nine pigs, seven sheep, one hundred pullets, one hundred pigeons, thirty capons and twenty hens, hares, rabbits, kids, salmon, eels, crabs, oysters, wild boars and red deer, was compensation for their journey.

cowhouses kept out of the metropolis.

Brown's dairy was demolished to make way for the Underground station, but moved to what was then 63 Parkway, on the north side very near the High Street junction, and had other branches in Albany Street. Its advertisement in the 1911 street directory still claimed to have been established in 1790.

William Bruges

Bruges (died c.1450) was appointed the first Garter King of Arms in 1415 – the most senior heraldic officer in an age when the registration and supervision of coats-of-arms developed. He lived, so far as can be judged, on the east side of St Pancras Way, by today's junction with Agar Grove. The house was moated and had its own chapel – in Bruges' will of 1449 he left some small candle-

Camden Civic Society

The Camden Civic Society is the direct descendant of the St Pancras Civic Society. The latter was formed on 1 July 1963, and the name was changed, well after the creation of Camden, in 1974, though it has to be said that the existence of strong environmental and preservation societies in Hampstead and Holborn has meant that the Camden Civic Society's sphere of activity has remained principally in the old St Pancras area.

The St Pancras society began with a protest by the artist Tammo de Yongh against the ugly lampposts erected near his house in Kentish Town. His anger at the lack of visual sensitivity often displayed by council officials struck a chord in a wider area, particularly in Camden Town where, eventually, the Society had its strongest nucleus. One early triumph was against the proposal to build a 16-storey block of flats at the junction of Primrose Hill Road and Ainger Road – it was reduced to 6 storeys. But it was not able to prevent the demolition of the south side of Oakley Square which has left us with an exceptionally dreary local authority development, nor could it prevent the tall blocks being built at Ampthill Square in **Bedford New Town**. Even with the aid of illustrious names and the Victorian Society it was not able to prevent the disgraceful destruction of handsome villas in Gloucester Avenue and their replacement by the dreadful Darwin Court.

The problem for all Camden conservation groups was that Camden's planning director, Bruno Schlaffenberg, really did want to demolish much of the ordinary, unspectacular housing and replace it with modern, preferably local authority, development, not necessarily tower blocks which, to be fair to him, were mostly planned before he was director.

The Society's role was eased by the introduction of conservation areas and, indeed, the multiple growth of very local residents' associations who could add their unified dissent against awful proposals.

Camden family and estate

Camden Town is mainly composed of the land which once belonged to two medieval manors – **Cantelowes** to the east of today's High Street, and the **Tottenhall** manor to the west. Much of Cantelowes was owned *c.*1670 by the Jeffreys family. A descendant, Elizabeth, daughter of Nicholas Jeffreys, married Charles Pratt (1714-94), who became 1st Earl Camden, taking his title from his seat, Camden Place, in Chislehurst. That in its turn had derived its name from William Camden, the Eliza-

31. Charles Pratt, 1st Earl Camden; portrait probably by Nathaniel Dance, in the later 1760s.

bethan historian and teacher, who moved there in 1609. Development began in 1791 and it was immediately known as Camden Town.

Charles Pratt (1714-94) was the most noted lawyer of his age, achieving popularity for his upholding of civil liberties, especially by opposing the continued prosecution of John Wilkes, and the taxation of American colonists. He was rewarded by being appointed Lord Chancellor in 1766, and having Camden County in Georgia, USA, named after him in 1777. He was made a baron in 1765. His son, John Jeffreys Pratt (1759-1840) was less tolerant of civil liberty, causing an uprising in Ireland when Lord Lieutenant there for his opposition to Catholic emancipation. Despite that he was created a Marquess in 1812. Much of Camden Town was developed during his lifetime.

A good number of local street names are related to the Camden family, including Jeffreys Street, Pratt Street and Bayham Street (a Camden estate in Kent), and Brecknock Road, from Brecknock Priory, owned by Camden's wife's family.

The Camden Town land had been part of the Prebendal holdings of St Paul's Cathedral, and so we have Prebend Street and St Paul's Crescent: **Agar** Grove was once called St Paul's Road. The Rev. Thomas Randolph was a St Paul's prebendary, and the builder of much of the early estate was Augustine Greenland though St Augustine's Road was probably named after the reputed founder of Old St Pancras Church. Marquis Road reflects the raising of John Jeffreys Pratt to be Marquess of Camden. George, the second marquess,

32. *Camden Goods Yard, probably in the 1920s.*

33. *A fire at Camden Goods Yard in 1857, sketched from Primrose Hill.*

married Harriet Murray the daughter of the Bishop of Rochester. His sister, Georgiana, has a street named after her, and Carol Street is named from another sister, Caroline.

Camden Goods Yard

A goods yard associated with the London & North-Western Railway (previously the London & Birmingham) developed at Camden Town when the railway bought the land between Chalk Farm Road and Gloucester Avenue, south from Chalk Farm station to the Regent's Canal. A long yellow-brick wall (eventually much blackened and once a prominent feature of Chalk Farm Road), was built to keep out trespassers. Some of this wall has been demolished in recent years, particularly with the building of a supermarket and housing.

Within the yard trains were

34. A prospect of **Gilbeys'** buildings at Camden Goods Yard in 1896. In the right foreground the large building is a bottle warehouse in Jamestown Road. To its left is the Stanhope Arms, demolished later to make way for the Gilbey headquarters built by **Chermayeff**. The Roundhouse in the distance was a Gilbey store and the sheds to the left are despatch warehouses for Gilbey.

maintained and goods handled amidst a large array of railway tracks and sheds, not to mention facilities for hundreds of horses. In addition to this yard operated by the railway the large firm of carriers, **Pickford's**, originally based at the City Road Basin on the canal, built their main warehouse south of the canal at the northern end of Oval Road. This building of 1841, which could take goods off both the canal and the railway, was later owned and rebuilt by **Gilbeys'**, the distillers.

The main railway goods yard sheds were immediately north of the canal and when rebuilt in 1864 were the largest such sheds in the country. By the end of the nineteenth century an 'Interchange' building had been built, constructed above a railway goods shed, but also with access to the canal, so that goods could be moved from one form of transport to another, or else on to road vehicles.

Goods traffic ceased in the 1960s just as it did later at the King's Cross yard, leaving two enormous areas for redevelopment in the area. At Camden the 15-acre site was owned by the National Freight Corporation which, through its property arm Hyperion, proposed to develop as housing for profitable sale, while Camden Council wanted to acquire it for social housing. An initial plan was to build a road from opposite Ferdinand Street, beneath the rail tracks, to emerge in Oval Road, but this did not happen because it meant the demolition of a listed building. Development was always going to be difficult. Not only were there

two railway lines going through the yard, but there were a number of listed buildings including the **Interchange Building**, the Stables and the rest of the so-called Stanley Sidings, the Horse Hospital, the **Roundhouse** and the vaults of the old stationary engine house, which had once pulled the trains up from Euston. Furthermore much of the available land had been considerably raised using clay from the Primrose Hill railway tunnel and was much higher than Chalk Farm Road.

In the event community housing was built in the Juniper Crescent development (the name deriving from one of the constituents of Gilbeys' gin) and at Gilbeys' Yard by the canal in the southern part of the site. This attractive development, which has about 200

27

35. *The cosy and informal Wine Inn at 159 Camden High Street. A drawing by Heather Peri c.1965. Soon after this date the bar closed and the building was joined in a particularly crass way to no. 161.*

Street buildings, except for a few premises along the lane called Britannia Row (today's Parkway), and some along Pratt Street and Crowndale Road. Two other old pubs on the west side are the **Britannia** and what became the Southampton Arms, opposite the **Cobden Statue**; this is nowadays called The Crescent. The west side of the road, on the Southampton estate was partially built up by the time that the Camden estate began its own development as from 1791 on the east side.

The High Street's previous character as a general shopping street has been transformed since the 1980s (*see* **Camden Markets**). There are some reminders of old businesses, one of which, J A Lake,

36. Pages' the butchers at 229-31 Camden High Street in the early 20th century.

homes for rent, was opened in 1997, and was designed by Peter Mason and Judith Tranter.

Camden High Street

The High Street stretches from Mornington Crescent Underground station to Camden Lock. It is an old road, being the route from the west end of London and the City up to Hampstead, but until the last quarter of the 18th century hardly any buildings were to be seen here except for the Mother Red Cap pub (now the World's End) and the Black Cap (previously on the site of the Underground station). Both of these are, confusingly, sometimes in the records called **Halfway House** – halfway between the West End and Hampstead. Thompson's map of *c.*1800 shows only fields behind both sides of the High

37. Wale's tea and coffee dealers at no. 235 Camden High Street c.1904.

the jewellers, is still at no. 33, and the tool and hardware merchant, Romany's at 52-6, founded by Frank Romany in 1920; the business was sold by the family in the mid-1980s. Sidney Bolsom, bootmaker and former mayor of St Pancras, still has his initials above 135. The building at nos. 197-209 that housed the main Camden Town drapers, Marshall Roberts, was used by the Co-op from the late 1940s.

One important part of Camden Town's history was at no. 80, where the firm of printers R & J Widdicombe had close association with the Conservative party on St Pancras council. Here they published the *St Pancras Gazette* in 1866, which later developed into the *Camden Journal* in 1965. This paper closed in 1980 after a long industrial dispute and it was bought for £1 by Eric Gordon who founded with partners the free paper **Camden New Journal** in 1982, which is now at 40 Camden Road. Trill's, the stationers, at 78 was one of the last of the old retailers to close. Harold Trill, later a mayor of St Pancras (as was his son), established the business in 1903 and it traded here until the mid 1980s. 'Trills for typewriters' was as familiar a sign as the neon-lit 'Alfred Kemp can fit anybody', further down the road near the Camden Palace – a claim that was almost the first thing to be seen from a bus entering Camden Town.

Apart from those already mentioned, most old pub names, if not the buildings, have disappeared. The Princess Beatrice is now Tommy Flynn's, The Wheatsheaf at the corner with Plender Street, is Belushi's bar and restaurant and the Camden Head at no. 100 is Liberties.

Camden Literary and Scientific Institution

The 1830s and 1840s were the heyday for the formation of organizations in London that wished to spread knowledge of both literature and science. Generally these attracted middle class or trades people, but they were accompanied also by the spread of mechanics' institutes. There were several Literary and Scientific Institutions locally. One was the Athenaeum, opposite Holloway Prison at the apex of Camden Road and Parkhurst Road; another was in Almeida Street, Islington (now the Almeida Theatre), and the one in Highgate Village, formed in 1839, still flourishes.

The fledgling Camden Town institution preceded Highgate Village in this. Seven local gentlemen met at a house opposite today's Sainsbury's in June 1835 to form a provisional committee and to make possible the printing of leaflets. The organization hired rooms at 40 Camden High Street, the membership grew to 80 and there was co-operation with the St Pancras Institution with a view to a merger. By 1836 lectures were being given in rooms in Pratt Street belonging to the local Paving Commissioners.

The venture was not a success. Membership had reduced by 1838 and in 1839 only 13 members renewed their subscriptions. Those left decided to discontinue the Institution.

(For a fuller account see Roger Cline, *Camden History Review* 21, 1997)

Camden Lock

Camden Lock, now synonymous with **Camden Markets** is a rich collection of industrial archaeology. Its beginnings were not propitious. When the **Regent's Canal** was built there was a great need to conserve water, since each time a lock is used water is lost to the lower level. An innovatory lock, devised by Sir William Congreve (1772-1828), was experimented with at Camden Town during the canal's construction which simply did not work. After a great deal of expense and the loss of four years, the canal company installed instead three locks that were less original and Camden Lock was opened on 12 August 1816, at that time the end of the navigable route from Paddington.

Diagonally across the canal here is what is known as the Roving Bridge. It was, explains *Streets of Camden Town*, "used by horses towing barges from the north bank to the south lock, and vice versa. It crossed the water diagonally so as to minimize the gradient that the horses had to negotiate."

The canal company had planned a number of depots along its route to enable loading and offloading. These included **Cumberland Basin** on a spur of the canal to the east of Albany Street, Battlebridge Basin at King's Cross, and Wenlock and City Road Basins, so that Camden Lock was not regarded then as an important wharfage area. However the Lock became much more significant when the **London & North Western Railway** (then the London & Birmingham) terminated its goods traffic near the canal at Camden Town in 1837 (*see* **Camden Goods Yard** *and* **Regent's Canal** *entries*).

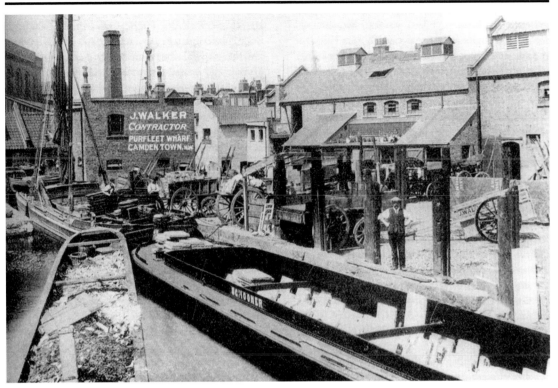

38. *Walker's Purfleet Wharf at Camden Lock, probably in 1911. This became Dingwall's Lock. Walker was a general cartage contractor, specialising in sand and ballast. A variety of craft are shown – a small sailing barge, a wide-beam open barge schooner and a narrow boat.*

Some kind of inter-transport facility existed before the present **Interchange Building** was built as from 1896. Now Grade II listed, this massive 5-storey building was used to switch goods between canal, railway and road. Above the open railway level there are three floors of warehouse – the original crane is still there. Beneath the building are vaults which for many years were used by Gilbeys' to store liquor, and there is a **horse tunnel** which links **Oval Road** to the Stables. The Interchange Basin itself could contain a number of barges or narrow boats at any one time. The building is now occupied mainly by media companies.

A basin and a yard were formed at the lock. This was known as Purfleet Wharf by the beginning of the 20th century, owned by contractor J. Walker. Its most famous proprietor, however, was T E Dingwall, maker of packing cases, who relocated here from the City Road Basin in the 1930s. Manufacture took place in the main building, and horses were kept in the stables that now house a large number of market stalls. Dingwall would be surprised to find his name perpetuated in a well-known bar and music place. The lock keeper's house is now a Starbuck's café which is also supposed to be a minimal information centre. John Le Carré in his *Tinker, Tailor, Soldier, Spy* thriller featured a 'safe house', where the denouement took place, at Camden Lock Cottages.

Camden Markets

The markets of Camden High Street and Chalk Farm Road have transformed Camden Town in the past twenty-five years. Beloved of young people and especially of tourists, they are now one of the country's biggest attractions, touted on the internet and tour buses. The markets have also affected the nature of the shops in the vicinity, and what was once a workaday, rather run down high street has been turned, at least at its northern end, into a profitable, jostling, lively and colourful assembly of stores, stalls and pavement sellers. In the wake of these has come a remarkable nightlife.

Most of the market activity is in the northern section of the High Street, between Camden

39. Camden Lock Market, by Hilda Bernstein.

use by Peter Wheeler and Bill Fullwood (joined later by Eric Reynolds). With minimal investment they could open a stall market which, if need be, could be wrapped up and closed without too much loss of capital. As Northside Developments Ltd in 1971 they bought the lease on the workshop buildings, formerly Dingwall's the premises of packing case manufacturers. The market stalls then had an emphasis on crafts, and the stables were rented by working crafts people. Good food was added to the attractions when Mother Huff's opened, and other stalls offered alternative foods that were rare in London. Dingwall's was converted to a bar and music spot in 1973, and became *the* place at weekends, crowded, hot and smokey.

The vitality of Camden Lock Market affected the area around. Where better to sell off-the-wall clothes than in the stretch leading from the tube station, the route of thousands of visitors to the Lock. Blatantly flouting planning laws, shopfronts were decorated with large three-dimensional objects that advertised, just as once did hanging shop signs to the illiterate, the trade within.

The Stables Market immediately to the north of Camden Lock is beneath the old goods yard and the main line. Much of this was once taken up by stables for the hundreds of horses that led their dark lives in this industrial area, but in later years once horse-power was redundant, it was taken by Gilbeys' for more storage space for their wines and spirits. Nowadays these rather run-down premises have been taken for yet more market stalls and boutiques, selling vintage clothes, ephemera, furniture, jewelry, collectors' items etc.

Town Underground and beyond the canal bridge, where the road becomes Chalk Farm Road. The southern stretch, down to Mornington Crescent, is relatively untouched by the rampant pop culture up the road: its own small market, in a section of Plender Street, and mainly fruit-and-veg, is a remnant of the street market that once ran along much of the High Street before traffic necessitated a cull and removal. Inverness Street market, opposite the Underground, is another older market (1901), mainly fruit-and-veg, but the attendant

shops have been absorbed into the culture of the clothes and jewelry stalls nearby.

The genesis of the market revolution was Camden Lock. This collection of derelict stables, yard and workshops by the canal was threatened with demolition with the coming of the proposed **Motorway Box**. Opposition to this disastrous proposal was prolonged but in the meantime, of course, sites such as Camden Lock were blighted and had no chance of substantial investment. It was the temporary nature of the Lock site that determined its

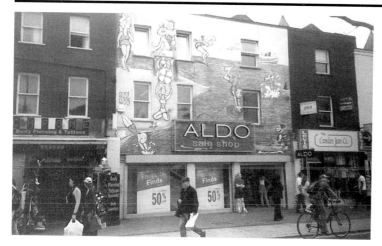

40 & 41. *Decorated shop fronts in Camden High Street in 2007.*

Camden New Journal

Camden Town's local newspaper arose from the ashes of the *Camden Journal* which closed down in 1980 after a period of industrial unrest. Eric Gordon, a former journalist and two others on the *Journal*, bought the title for £1 and in 1982 launched the *Camden New Journal* on a borrowed capital of £50,000. It was at first a modest free sheet, but of later years it is an essential local paper, that now has a sister publication in Islington.

Camden New Town

This name applied to the area encompassed by St Pancras Way and York Way on west and east, and by Agar Grove and Camden Road on south and north. The streets here were mostly developed in the second phase of the making of Camden Town, by then in the ownership of George Pratt, 2nd Marquess of Camden. Building

42. *A semi-detached villa at 187 Camden Road, beginning of the 20th century.*

There are about 350 stalls or shops here, many of them housed in brick arches beneath the main railway line.

On the other side of Chalk Farm Road the nature of the shops has also changed. Thirty years ago it was an assembly of rather down-at-heel second-hand furniture shops, but it is now much smarter and wider in its appeal.

By the road bridge, adjacent to the canal, is the Regent's Canal Market. A new building development in The Stables Market is scheduled to start at the end of 2007, and will sub-stantially change its character.

What used to be called Buck Street market is between the canal and the tube station on the east side of the main road. A further 200 stalls are here, many selling own design jewelry and clothing. This market has an uncertain future, as the site is part of a plan by Transport for London to develop the Underground station. Also with a question mark is that market which functions at times in the premises of the **Electric Ballroom**, also threatened by the underground station proposals.

43. Camden Square, c.1905

44. Camden Road, early 20th century.

45. A dilapidated 81 Camden Road in the 1970s.

was gradual, from about 1834 to 1871, and the properties more spacious than the terraces of the first phase of building to the east of Camden High Street. The principal developments were along Camden Road and the creation of **Camden Square** with its central church of St Paul's. Camden Road, a turnpike road which had been proposed by the Hampstead and Highgate Turnpike Trust, was begun in 1824 and finished in 1827 as part of a route from the West End to Tottenham. It was lined with substantial villas, many of them unfortunately lost in recent times, though there are enough left to imagine the earlier scene. Horse buses used the route in the 1830s, thereby encouraging development along it.

Camden School for Girls

The school now occupies extensive premises in Sandall Road, but its origins lie in a terrace-house in Camden Street, then numbered 46, but later 12-14. Here, on 4 April 1850, Frances Mary Buss, 23-year-old daughter of an artist and engraver, opened her **North**

47. The first premises of the North London Collegiate School for Girls and of the Camden School for Girls, in Camden Street.

46. Frances Mary Buss, founder of North London Collegiate School for Girls, and the Camden School for Girls.

London Collegiate School for Ladies. It was a significant day for the education of women in this country, for it was her policy to educate girls to the standard enjoyed by middle-class boys. This seemingly innocuous aim was in advance of its time, for it was the almost invariable fate of girls in middle class homes to rely for an education on a governess or the resources of their own homes. If they were poorer they were sent to dame or charity schools where their education was directed to preparing them to become housewives or domestic servants.

Miss Buss's school was successful and she became a celebrated name in the educational world, for, with others, she pressed for the right of women to sit for degrees and attend university.

Her school outgrew the premises in Camden Street and moved on to Camden Road but she was not content with this success. She knew that a great many girls of working class or lower middle-class parents, unable to pay even the modest fees of the North London Collegiate, also needed the sort of education she provided. In January 1871 the Camden School for Girls opened in the vacant Camden Street premises. Miss Buss was able to report that 40 girls turned up on the first day, and that their fathers "included clerks, tailors and civil servants as well as two builders, two grocers and two clergymen; there was also an engineer in the British Museum, a cattle salesman, a boarding-house keeper, an accountant, a bootmaker, an inspector of police ... and a dealer in works of art." By May of that year the school had 112 girls on the roll, and by 1876 there were 356. In 1878, again with the need for a larger building, the school moved to the former Governesses' Benevolent Institution in Prince of Wales Road, Kentish Town. Meanwhile, the North London Collegiate had opened a new building in Sandall Road, which it left in 1938.

It was not until 1956 that the Camden School for Girls could move to Sandall Road to succeed the Collegiate School there.

48. *St Paul's church in Camden Square, c.1905.*

The building had been badly damaged in the war, money was very tight and at times the prospects were hopeless. The new school was officially opened on 18 October 1956.

Since then Camden has become one of the most notable schools in the area, and now also takes boys at sixth-form level.

Camden Square

The Square, built from the 1840s, was the centrepiece of **Camden New Town**, a renewed attempt by the Camden family to make money out of its fields after the less-than-enthu-siastic response to its initial development to the east of the High Street. St Paul's church was built in the square in 1847-49 before many of the antici-pated congregation had ar-rived. It was designed by F W Ordish and J Johnson, and a parish hall, designed by Arthur Blomfield, followed in 1900. The church was bombed dur-ing the Second World War and demolished, apart from the tower and spire in 1949. The rest of the building was taken down in 1956. The parish hall survived the bombing and af-ter the war the parish was merged with that of St Luke's in Oseney Crescent, where-upon a new parish hall and chapel were erected on the site in Camden Square. Now that St Luke's is redundant, St Paul's undistinguished chapel is once again the parish church.

Today, most of the houses on the north-west side have been lost and replaced by apartment blocks quite out of keeping, architecturally.

Streets of Camden Town notes that the rules for the Camden Square gardens forbade 'bois-terous or dangerous games... such as cricket, football, round-ers, hockey, skipping with long ropes, trundling iron hoops, and shooting bows and ar-rows...' The residents of that day would therefore be sur-prised to find that a good part of the open space is today taken up by an adventure play-ground, one of the earliest in the country, opened in the 1950s by St Pancras Council.

A remarkable feature once of the square on the site of the playground, was a small meteorological station. This was installed by friends of George James Symons (1838-1900), who moved to no. 62 Camden Square in 1868. Symons was particularly inter-ested in the study of rainfall, and formed the British Rainfall Association whose members contributed to a long weather record. By 1899 there were nearly 2900 meteorological sta-tions involved in his enterprise throughout England and Wales, with more in Scotland and Ireland. His own station was in his back garden at no. 62. After his death the house remained the headquarters of the Association and the home of his 14,000 books on meteor-ology, but the station in his gar-den was removed to the square gardens.

Symons was twice president

49. *Frederick Goodall RA in his studio.*

Montague Holl (1845-88), artist, here from about 1877-82. A modern artist, Tess Jaray (1937) was at no. 29 in 1973, and the conductor Sir Charles Groves (1915-92) was here at the time of his death.

A plaque has been fixed on no. 57 commemorating the residence of the Indian politician and St Pancras councillor, **Krishna Menon**. However, he appears to have lived instead at 7 Camden Terrace, a row of Italianate villas which forms the north side of the square, from 1938 until 1947, when he returned to India for the coming of Indian independence.

Camden Theatre

The theatre at the corner of the High Street and Crowndale Road was opened as the Royal Camden Theatre on 26 December, 1900 by the actor Ellen Terry – in time for the seasonal *Cinderella* pantomime. Miss Terry's appearance here is still marked by a plaque in the theatre entrance. Camden Theatre was built in the heyday of theatre construction, and designed by one of the most famous theatre architects, W G R

of the Royal Meteorological Society, whose highest award, the Symons Memorial Gold Medal, bears his name.

The **London Irish Centre** occupies premises at the southern corner of the square with Murray Street.

Famous residents have included Sir Lawrence Alma-Tadema (1836-1912), the Dutch-born artist, who briefly rented 4 Camden Square from another artist, Frederick Goodall, from September 1870 until May 1871, after which he moved on to St John's Wood. Goodall (1822-1904) was one of the most prolific and successful artists of his time. When the Royal Academy held an exhibition in 1869, Goodall showed 50 pictures, all of which were immediately purchased by the art dealer Ernest Gambart who then resold all of them for £6,000 before the end of the exhibition. By this time Goodall was earning about £10,000 a year, a vast sum for an artist. He was intermittently at Camden Square until 1870, but spent much of his time travelling. Also at this address were Francis Holl (1815-84), engraver, and his son Frank

50. *Ellen Terry who opened and also appeared at the Camden Theatre.*

51. *The Camden Theatre c.1905.*

Sprague, in a 'free classic' style, featuring a number of statues on the parapet. Estimates of its seating capacity vary widely, but it was most likely just over 2,400.

"The new theatre at once strikes the visitor as a lofty and commanding edifice", wrote one journalist. A marble staircase led to a crush room furnished with deep red upholstery and decorated by Waring & Gillow in Louis XIV style. The sight lines were excellent: "...an excellent view of the stage can be obtained from all parts of the house, which is on the two-tier cantilever principle, dress-circle and balcony on the first tier, and an amphitheatre and gallery on the second." Electricity as well as gas lit the theatre. The interior of the domed roof was painted with allegorical figures representing the twenty-four hours,

by a Mr Arthur Black, who taught at the Camden School of Art.

The ensuing productions were a mix of straight drama and melodrama, plus light opera such as *The Geisha* in 1901. The *St Pancras Gazette* was fulsome: "On Monday the ever-popular *Geisha* commenced on a too-brief run of six nights at the Camden Theatre, and has had a week of most gratifying success. It is a matter for special gratification that the opera was presented at our beautiful local theatre on a scale of magnificence and completeness which would do credit to a West End theatre, but this is nothing new at the Camden Theatre...." Such successes did not prevent the Camden becoming a variety theatre, called the Camden Hippodrome, by 1909.

In 1913 the building was in

52. *Events advertised at the Camden Theatre in 1904.*

53. *A programme cover for the Camden Theatre, c.1920.*

use as a cinema, and it closed sometime during the Second World War. Probably it survives only because the BBC took it over for orchestral concerts from 1945 until 1972, a period in which many 'redundant' theatre buildings in London were torn down without too much opposition.

Subsequently it has been a nightclub and home to pop bands: Nero's, then Music Machine, then Camden Palace, and now Koko's.

Camden Town Group

Camden Town's most notable contribution to British art was built upon the friendship between **Walter Sickert** (1860-1942) and Spencer Gore (1878-1914). By 1907 Sickert, then flourishing at 19 Fitzroy Street in Fitzrovia, was the leading light of a coterie of Post-Impressionist artists very much at war with the art establishment. Gore, renewing acquaintance

with Sickert, joined the group, which also consisted of Harold Gilman, Robert Bevan and Charles Ginner. Gore lived then at 18 Fitzroy Street, moving in 1907 to Granby Terrace opposite Mornington Crescent and then in 1912, with his new wife to 2 Houghton Place nearby.

The Fitzroy group evolved into the Camden Town Group, of which Gore was elected president in 1911. Members, other than the original group, were Walter Bayes, Augustus John, Henry Lamb, Wyndham Lewis, James Manson and Lucien Pissarro.

The Camden Town Group was short-lived, for by 1911 it had evolved into the London Group which itself was a merger of the Camden Town Group and the Vorticists.

The Camden Town Murder

A seemingly run-of-the-mill murder in 1907 became a celebrated case and still today nurtures a wealth of conjecture and literature. On 12 September that year a prostitute, Emily Dimmock, was found with her throat cut at what is now 29 Agar Grove (then St Paul's Road). She lodged there with her common-law husband, Bert Shaw, a railway restaurant-car cook who worked nights – this left Emily, of course, the opportunity to pursue her old trade in the locality. Shaw was suspected of the crime, but no charges were brought since he was on a train at the time. Instead, another man known to Emily, Robert Wood, a glassware designer, was arrested and charged. He was eventually acquitted, and the murderer was never found.

The crime itself is not so noteworthy or bizarre to have

Daily Mirror

See To-day's 'DAILY MAIL.'

THE MORNING JOURNAL WITH THE SECOND LARGEST NET SALE.

No. 1,286. Registered at the G.P.O. as a Newspaper. FRIDAY, DECEMBER 13, 1907. One Halfpenny.

CAMDEN TOWN MURDER MYSTERY: ROBERT WOOD ON TRIAL FOR HIS LIFE AT THE NEW BAILEY.

The curtain rose on the third act in the Camden Town murder drama yesterday when Robert Wood, an artist, was put in the dock at the Central Criminal Court and tried for the murder of Emily Dimmock on the night of September 11. (1) Robert Wood, the accused man. (2) Emily Dimmock, the murdered woman. (3) Ruby Young, the accused man's sweetheart, who is the principal witness for the prosecution. (4) Mr. Marshall Hall, the leading counsel for the defence. (5) Mr. Arthur Newton, the prisoner's solicitor, who prepared the defence, and who defended Wood during the magisterial hearing. (6) The crowd outside the New Bailey watching the entrance of Ruby Young, who is under one of the umbrellas seen in the photograph. (7) Mr. Justice Grantham, the presiding Judge. (8) Sir Charles Mathews, who is prosecuting on behalf of the Crown. (Elliott and Fry, Greswell, Bassano, and London Stereoscopic.)

54. Press coverage of the murder in Agar Grove in 1907. Top left is the defendant, Robert Wood, and top right Emily Dimmock, the victim. Centre is Ruby Young, a girlfriend of the accused. Marshall Hall, the barrister for the defence is to her left.

55. Agar Grove (then St Paul's Road) c.1905.

made it famous. A number of other circumstances have done that. Firstly, Wood's defending counsel was the famous Sir Edward Marshall Hall, whose melodramatic approach to courtroom procedure appealed to juries but nowadays would be slapped down by judges. But he made good headlines, especially at a time when the tabloid press was nearly as prurient and sensational as it is today. Also, Wood was the first defendant in a murder trial, since the Criminal Justice Act of 1905, to be able to defend himself in the witness box. And then in 1908 artist **Walter Sickert** produced a number of pictures featuring the subject. All these things, together with the general seediness of the situation (and indeed of Camden Town) appealed to the public's appetite for violent scandal.

Recently the murder came back into the news with a book by the American crime writer, Patricia Cornwell, who sought to connect Sickert, the Camden Town Murder and, more sensationally, the Jack the Ripper murders of nearly twenty years earlier.

Camden Town Underground station

The Underground station at the apex of Kentish Town Road and Camden High Street is today threatened by demolition and redevelopment. In its present form it is inadequate for the crowds of a normal weekday let alone for those which descend on the **Camden Markets** each weekend, and certainly the interior could do with regeneration. However, the plan is to replace this modest, ox-blood tiled building, designed by Leslie Green, with a vast office block to maximize the site value.

The site of the station is by Camden Town standards, an old one. The government in 1776 announced a plan to erect gallows here, but this was not proceeded with. The Mother Black Cap, or **Halfway House**, stood here in the 18th century – the Mother Red Cap was just across the road and is now the World's End. The Black Cap building was used in 1778 for the second St Pancras **Workhouse**. However, the vestry true to form provided too small a house for the poor, and by 1787 it was very overcrowded. In the meantime, the Mother Black Cap pub was reopened on the west side of the High Street. Eventually, the triangular site was occupied by shops, including **Brown's Dairy**, but in 1903 it was bought by the Charing Cross, Euston and Hampstead Railway Company as the site for their key station here.

When first built the extent of what became part of the Northern Line was from the Strand up to Camden Town, and then by two arms to Golders Green and to Archway (then called

56. A diagramatic illustration of what became the Northern Line, branching north from Camden Town.

Highgate). Camden Town station was therefore V-shaped, with one line beneath Camden High Street and the other beneath Kentish Town Road. South and northbound trains are double decked so that there are only two tunnels. This was to avoid having to tunnel beneath buildings and possible compensation.

The tube station was opened on 22 June 1907 by Lloyd George.

Cantelowes Manor

Camden Town was part of the old parish and borough of St Pancras. More precisely, it was originally part of the two manors of Cantelowes to the east of the High Street and **Tottenhall** to the west. Cantelowes stretched from Highgate village, east of Highgate Road and Kentish Town Road, down to the present Agar Grove. Eastwards it extended to the old road now represented by Dartmouth Park Hill, Brecknock Road and York Way – the parish boundary with Islington. The site of the manor house is uncertain, but most probably it was just north of today's Agar Grove by St Pancras Way, but the records do not make clear which side of the road it was on.

From early medieval times the manor belonged to a Prebend of St Paul's Cathedral, but was seized by Parliament in the 1640s. About 1670 the copyhold rights of the manor were sold to the Jeffreys family. An heiress, Elizabeth Jeffreys, married Charles Pratt who became 1st Earl Camden, and thus Cantelowes became part of Camden's estates.

Manors held sway over much local activity until the 18th century. Cantelowes

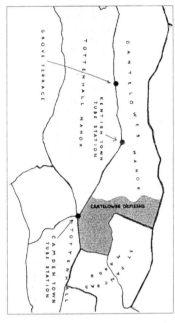

57. An approximate depiction of the boundaries of St Pancras manors. Cantelowes manor is to the east.

manor had two courts of administration, the Court Baron which dealt with the transfer of copyhold property belonging to the Lord of the Manor, and the Court Leet which regulated the upkeep of roads, tracks and waterways, dealt with minor crime, appointed officers to maintain highways, test ale, and make sure that poor people from outside the parish did not settle here and become a charge on the ratepayers.

Gradually the functions of the manor were absorbed by the parish vestry which was empowered to raise rates, in particular for the upkeep of the poor. Though in theory the manor continued well into the 20th century, it had by then no power in the governance of the area, although until the abolition of its court baron powers it could still meet to record changes of land ownership. The extant court rolls date from the 15th century.

Cantelowes Road is a reminder of the manor, just as Prebend Street and St Paul's Crescent echo its previous ownership by St Paul's Cathedral – Agar Grove was once St Paul's Road. The Cantelowes Archers were founded in 1849 and used space in Camden Square gardens to practise.

58. Carreras factory and headquarters in the 1920s (see p. 44).

59. An early Carreras Craven 'A' advertisement.

Carreras

Dominating the northern end of Hampstead Road, just south of Mornington Crescent station, is Greater London House, a handsome white building with Egyptian motifs and two large bronze black cats outside. This is the former factory of Carreras, the cigarette makers (the name is still emblazoned at roof-top level), whose best known brands were Craven 'A' and Black Cat. In an exhaustive search into the background of the firm, David Hayes has discovered that the Carreras family settled in the area of Somers Town and Camden Town after members had fled the despotic regime installed in Spain in the 1820s. The business of cigar making was led by José Joaquin Carreras who by 1861 had a shop in Soho, patronized by Edward VII, and also by the 3rd Earl of Craven, a pipe smoker for whom Carreras developed a 'Craven

mixture', a name later to be used in the filter-tip brand of Craven 'A', still sold by British American Tobacco.

The business was sold in 1896 to an American, William Johnston Yapp, who in 1903 joined forces with a Russian, Bernhard Baron whose firm, the Baron Cigarette Machinery Co. marketed a machine that made cigarettes at the rate of 18,000 per hour – this dramatically outpaced the speed at which a woman worker could hand roll cigarettes. The firm expanded and prospered and eventually opened a new factory in City Road, called the Arcadia Works and, tacitly acknowledging that smoking could damage your health, was the first firm to develop a cork tip to soak up the worst of the pollutants. Inevitably, as sales grew, a new factory was wanted.

The site of this was the garden ground of Mornington Crescent which had been sold for development against strong protest. The architects of the new Arcadia Works were M E and O H Collins, who capitalized on the interest aroused by the recently opened Tutankhamun tomb, and based their design on a temple at Bubastis, which featured the cat-headed god Bastet. The factory, built by McAlpine's, was opened in 1928. There were 3000 employees, most of them women. About 1960, by which time the firm had been bought by Rembrandt Tobacco Company, parts of the operation were transferred to new premises in Basildon. Two thirds of the employees went at the same time, and as David Hayes has discovered, one of the black cats which adorned the outside went as well, and the other to Jamaica.

On the departure of Carreras the building was converted into offices called Greater London House, many of them taken by the Greater London Council and a large advertising agency. The renovation of 1998-9 was the work of the new owners, Revolution Property.

(See David Hayes, 'Carreras: family, firm and factory' in *Camden History Review* 27, 2003).

Barbara Castle

A number of well-known people have been councillors for Camden and its preceding components, St Pancras, Holborn and Hampstead. These include George Bernard Shaw, **Krishna Menon**, Ken Livingstone, Henry Brooke and Peter Brooke, Geoffrey Finsberg, Tessa Jowell, Frank Dobson and **Peggy Duff**. Another was Barbara Betts, better known later as Barbara Castle, who became a councillor for a ward which covered a part of Camden Town in 1937.

Barbara Betts (1910-2002) was born in Chesterfield to a left-wing family. After university and a mundane job in Manchester, she came to London in 1935 where she became involved in politics and, according to her autobiography, was frequently to be seen selling left-wing news-sheets outside Mornington Crescent station. A feminist and firm left-winger, she was a constant thorn in the side of the conservative Municipal Reform administration of St Pancras. Her aspirations led her to be adopted as a Parliamentary candidate and she was elected as MP for Blackburn in the landslide Labour victory in 1945.

She rose to become a senior figure in Parliament, keeping to

60. *The original villas on the site of Cecil Sharp House, c.1840 and probably built by Henry Bassett who designed villas nearby in Gloucester Avenue. The villa to the left was called Tower Villa and was later numbered as part of Regent's Park Road, and Tower House to the right was eventually numbered in Gloucester Avenue. Note the criss-cross motif in the wall, which is found still in the front walls of a number of houses in Regent's Park Road.*

the left of the Party and, in her latter years, as Baroness Castle, championing the cause of older people.

Cecil Sharp House

The home of the English Folk Dance and Song Society at the apex of Gloucester Avenue and Regent's Park Road was designed by H M Fletcher and formally opened in 1931 by the historian H A L Fisher. This replaced two large villas facing south, which the London & North Western Railway at one time wanted to demolish so as to erect some dwellings for railway workers. This plan was soon seen off by local residents.

The Society was formed in 1932 with the merger of the Folk-Song Society and the English Folk Dance Society. The former had been founded by

enthusiasts in 1898 and the collection and recording of folk songs was intensified under the leadership of Cecil Sharp (1859-1924) and Ralph Vaughan Williams. Sharp went on to found the English Folk Dance Society in 1911, of

61. *Cecil Sharp House in 2007.*

which he was the Director. It was after Sharp's death and upon the initiative of the new Director, Douglas Kennedy, that the two societies merged.

Centre 42

The formation of Centre 42 in 1964 at **The Roundhouse** probably saved that derelict building from destruction at a time when the conservation of industrial archaeology was not regarded as much of a priority – the magnificent Euston station and its Arch were destroyed only two years earlier.

The Centre derived its name from Article 42 passed by the Trades Union Congress in 1960 which asserted that art should be for everyone and as free as possible, a cause that was championed by playwright Arnold Wesker (b. 1932), who had helped steer the proposal to fruition at the TUC. Unfortunately, the component members of the TUC were less forthcoming in their subsequent donations and the Centre always struggled for money.

In 1964 businessman Louis Mintz gave the Centre the remaining 16-years' lease of The Roundhouse and therefore it was an assured home, even if an expensive conversion was necessary for it to be suitable for public performance. Wesker became artistic director and George Hoskins (whose other contribution to the culture of those years was the revival of coffee houses in London in the 1950s) was business manager. Wesker's view was that art should be "beyond the commercial world of entertainment and should be subsidized and not forced to pay for itself." This was not itself a new argument, but the problem was that donations and grants were hard

62. Arnold Wesker, founder of Centre 42. Photograph by Roger Mayne, 1958. © Roger Mayne/National Portrait Gallery, London.

to come by, despite a fund-raising reception held by Harold Wilson at No. 10 Downing Street.

Increasingly Wesker became disillusioned by the importation of high-profile productions on a rental basis and the diminution of his original purpose. During this period some notable productions took place, such as Peter Brook's *Tempest*, and these were joined by outstanding rock acts such as Pink Floyd, Fairport Convention, Jimi Hendrix, Otis Redding and The Doors. Kenneth Tynan's notorious *Oh Calcutta!*, celebrating both nudity and the end of the Lord Chamberlain's censorious powers, and Barrault's production of *Rabelais* also made headlines.

Wesker himself resigned in 1972, though Hoskins continued to keep The Roundhouse afloat. In 1977 Thelma Holt became Artistic Director and there was an increase in activity. She persuaded the Greater London Council to grant £120,000 per

annum, but it was still too little and in 1983 The Roundhouse and what was left of the Centre 42 project closed.

Chalcot Square

This irregularly-shaped square was first occupied 1849-1858. Some of its houses, stretch round into what is now Chalcot Road, but are architecturally part of the Square. It was first named St George's Square, no doubt to attract similarly patriotic residents as those of St George's Terrace nearby, which was built a few years earlier. Chalcot Road was once St George's Road. The London County Council, in its zest to eliminate street names that confusingly duplicated others, changed both names to their present form in 1937.

At number 3 in the early 1880s lived Frederick Furnivall (1825-1910), a well-known philologist. Not only was he one of the three founders of the *Oxford English Dictionary* but

63. *Chalcot Square in 2007.*

More famously, No. 7 was the brief home of the **poets** Ted Hughes (1930-98) and Sylvia Plath (1932-63). They were here from 1960 to 1962. Their marriage fell apart in the autumn of 1962, after which she moved to Fitzroy Road. During 1962 Sylvia Plath's output of poems was prodigious. Other well-known residents have included the broadcaster, Joan Bakewell.

Chalk Farm and Chalk Farm Tavern

The subsoil of the area is clay and the derivation of 'Chalk' Farm must be sought just further north where the Hampstead manor of Chalcots was owned by the St James's Leper Hospital (on the site of today's St James's Palace) until 1449 when it was granted to Eton College. Variations of the name, which means a shelter for travellers from cold weather, are

was also its editor from 1861 to 1870. However, his irascible and not very organized nature led to his acrimonious resignation. He was an inveterate founder of societies, ranging from the New Shakspere Society (as he insisted on spelling it), to societies devoted to the work of Browning and Chaucer; he was also secretary of the Philological Society from 1853 almost until his death. He left his wife of many years at the age of 58 and married a 21-year-old secretary, who died in a fire in their home in Lincolnshire.

64. *Chalcot Crescent c.1905, near Chalcot Square, and now much sought-after.*

65. Chalk Farm Tavern in 1815.

To be Lett
At Primrose Hill by
Hampstead Road,
Chalk-House, the Tile
Kiln and Stables, the
Materials and large
conveniences for Tile-
making, 13 acres of
Land, with Plenty of
strong Clay that will
make tiles to bear both
Frost and Rain.
Enquire of Mr Badcock
on the Pavement in
Moorfields, London.
From the London Evening
Post, 2 December 1740.

Chaldecote or Caldecote. The manor extended from Belsize almost to Regent's Park Road where stood Lower Chalcot's Farm, later known as Chalk House Farm and later still the Chalk Farm Tavern. Thus the area near to the tavern became known as Chalk Farm though residents and estate agents have conspired in modern times to rename it Primrose Hill.

The tavern first comes to notice in 1678 when the body of Sir Edmund Berry Godfrey, a London magistrate, was found face down, impaled by a sword, in a ditch at Primrose Hill. In fact he had been strangled and dumped there probably some

66. Chalk Farm Tavern in 1836. Watercolour by Edmund Marks.

days after his murder elsewhere. The crime was a famous one, committed at a time when Titus Oates was stoking the fires of his alleged Catholic conspiracy, and as Godfrey was involved with the Oates campaign Catholics were blamed for his murder. Though men were found guilty and hanged, the evidence against them seems insubstantial.

Godfrey's body was taken to the White House (later the Chalk Farm Tavern) described in House of Lords records as "an ale house, with no accommodation, nor hangings, nor scarce a glass window". The inn next appears in the Middlesex Licensing Records of 1732, and it is noted once more in 1751. By 1760 the place is called the Stag and Hounds; in 1790 it was licensed to Thomas Rutherford, whose name appears on the c.1800 map of the parish of St Pancras, and it was then called the Chalk Farm Tea Gardens. Rutherford's advertisement for his enterprise in 1793 claimed that his wines were real and the other liquors of a superior kind. Plus tea and rolls as usual.

An illustration of about that time shows the Tavern to have the almost obligatory Long Room at first floor level with views over Primrose Hill. By the 1860s the tavern, which had been rebuilt in its present form in the 1850s, could boast a dance floor said to be capable of taking 1000 people. This, set in the gardens opposite the front, occupied some valuable building land and the brewers, Calvert (hence Calvert Street nearby), sold them off so that the Sharpleshall Street/ Berkley Road/Regent's Park Road triangle could be built.

Early in the 1970s the name of the tavern became Pub Lotus, but later reverted to its old name, before becoming the Lemonia restaurant.

Chalk Farm Road

On Thompson's c.1800 detailed map of the parish of St Pancras, Chalk Farm Road has no name except being the road to or from Hampstead. There are no buildings and, at that time, no canal crossing at its southern end nor, of course, railway land to the west. This did not prevent, in 1971, an antique dealer called Harvey at nos 67-71 advertising that behind his shop's façade stood the original 'Chalk Farm' – a Queen Anne farmhouse no less, he asserted. Then again, James Bristow, a serious researcher into local history in the 1950s, identified No. 87 as the old Chalk Farm House. "One or two alterations have been made to adapt it to a commercial purpose, but the greater part of the building stands just as it was when it was erected in Queen Anne's reign. Its front door has gone, but the lintels and door post survive and its quaint staircase; and an old stone building at the back may

67. Chalk Farm Road, c.1905, taken from near the Roundhouse. In the background works are proceeding with the construction of Chalk Farm Station. A remnant of the horse trough still survives.

49

68. *The Railway Tavern at 35 Chalk Farm Road in 1905, a photograph taken before the tunnelling for the Northern Line beneath the road in front. It is on the corner with Harmood Street.*

abruptly terminated when the Revolution in Russia began. Undaunted, he became, according to Jack Whitehead in his book on Camden Town, a gigolo at grand London hotels or, as the *Dictionary of National Biography* discreetly describes him, a professional ballroom dancer and partner. He married in England and through his wife's connections he met Lord Waring who employed him in charge of modern design at Waring & Gillow, the famous furnishing business, where he pioneered Art Deco furniture. Chermayeff is best known for his De La Warr Pavilion at Bexhill, which he designed with Erich Mendelsohn in 1935. Gilbey House, the administrative headquarters of the **Gilbey** wines and spirits firm, which

have been the dairy. The garage next door was the old cowshed."

By 1834 the road was known as Pancras Vale and soon lined with terraces and gardens on the east side, and even some houses on the west, south of the Roundhouse, which were soon to be swept away as the goods depot expanded.

An interesting resident of Pancras Vale was Robert Benson Dockray (1811-70), resident engineer of the London & North Western Railway. He was the engineer, and possibly the architect, of the Roundhouse – his work on this is discussed in the **Roundhouse** entry.

Serge Chermayeff

Chermayeff (1900-96) designed an outstanding modernist building in Camden Town – what used to be Gilbey House (now Academic House) at the junction of Jamestown Road and Oval Road. Born in Chechnya but educated at Harrow, Chermayeff was unable to go to university as funds were

69. *Chermayeff's headquarters building for Gilbeys' at the corner of Oval Road and Jamestown Road. It replaced the Stanhope Arms.*

had numerous warehouses in the goods yard nearby (and in the **Roundhouse**), was completed in 1937. Chermayeff also worked closely on a number of projects with Jack Pritchard and Wells Coates who were responsible for the remarkable Lawn Road flats in Hampstead. Most of Chermayeff's later career was spent in the United States. At Yale he taught the young British students Richard Rogers and Norman Foster.

Cinemas

Moving pictures were being shown at the Bedford Theatre in Camden High Street before 1900, at a time when the young Cecil Hepworth (1874-1953) was beginning his own first film productions. As a child Hepworth lived at 37 St Paul's Crescent (now demolished), and later he and his family moved to 32 Cantelowes Road and then on to 45 St Augustine's Road, all streets near Camden Square. His father, who had dabbled in magic lantern displays, encouraged him to experiment in projecting moving images and in 1899 Cecil converted a room in his house in Walton-on-Thames and from here promoted a film company which broke new ground in filming the funeral of Queen Victoria in 1901. Hepworth achieved some fame in the British film making scene but his work lost out to more glamorous and inventive Hollywood productions, though he did introduce the very first 'film star' in the form of a collie dog.

The first permanent cinema in Camden Town was the Dara at 16-18 Delancey Street, later called The Fan, converted from a roller skating rink. Opened in 1908, it closed in 1917 and has

70. *The Plaza cinema in Camden High Street, now demolished.*

mostly since been a billiard hall. A year later the Electric Cinema opened at 211 Camden High Street in a converted bakery. In 1937 its foyer was redesigned by Cecil Massey in mock Tudor style and next year became the Plaza. Post-war its fortunes deteriorated until in 1977 it became an independent cinema run by Andy and Pam Engel showing art films. However, in 1994 it was virtually forced to close and developers proposed to demolish it and the Parkway cinema around the corner as part of a large development. This scheme foundered against public and borough council opposition, but still the Plaza in the late 1990s was replaced by a block that today contains offices and a Virgin megastore, designed by Chapman Taylor.

The most attractive cinema in Camden Town, at least in its interior features, was and is the Odeon in Parkway, variously known in the past as the Gaumont, Gate 3 and the Parkway. Its ups and downs

since it opened in 1937 on the site of the **Park Theatre** have been as various as its names, but its heyday was in the 1980s under the management of Peter Walker, when, refurbished to something like its former Art Deco glory, it won the affection and loyalty of a new audience which joined in the clamour opposed to its proposed destruction. The cinema closed in 1993 but was reopened as a multiplex Odeon in 1997. It is still open but its road frontage out of working hours is now a sorry sight – dirty and unadorned as though it has closed down altogether.

The original building was designed by W E and Sydney Trent and Daniel McKay.

The Avenue Picture Palace had a short life (1912-15) in Pratt Street in a converted Baptist chapel. The **Bedford Theatre** showed films for much of the 1930s and the **Camden Theatre** was a cinema from 1913 until *c*.1940.

(See Mark Aston, *The Cinemas of Camden* (1997) published by London Borough of Camden)

Cobden statue

The politician Richard Cobden (1804-65) had no known relationship with Camden Town, yet his rather ugly statue stands in a prominent position at the southern end of the High Street on the site of an old tollgate. He was a famous man at the time of his death, having worked tirelessly and detrimentally to his health in repealing the hated Corn Laws and bringing about free trade with France, thereby earning the gratitude of Napoleon III, who is said to have been a major donor in the statue's construction.

71. *The old toll house and gate on the site of the Cobden statue.*

72. *The Cobden Statue, c.1905.*

But why in Camden Town? It came about because of the enthusiasm of some local residents whom the *Camden & Kentish Town Gazette* noted had the 'spirited idea' to honour the late politician in 1865. Spirited or not, one of his sons-in-law emphasized that Cobden had no connection to the area, but in his view it was put there because a vacant space became available "and it was thought that it might as well be filled by a bad statue". The statue, executed in Sicilian marble by Wills Brothers of Euston Road and Kentish Town Road, was unveiled on 27 June 1868; it cost £320, collected from private subscriptions. Sheaves of corn on the sides of the Portland stone pedestal are a reminder of Cobden's campaign to abolish the Corn Laws.

Coincidentally, another of Cobden's sons-in-law (though posthumously), the painter **Walter Sickert**, at one time lived overlooking the statue. Sickert, moved to Mornington Crescent in 1908.

73. *Frederick Collard.*

74. *Muzio Clementi.*

Collard and Collard

Piano making was an important industry in Camden and Kentish Towns in the 19th century. Not only were there companies which put together instruments on assembly lines, but numerous craftsmen working from home and small workshops making components. They flourished as the possession of a piano (with the absence of other means to provide home music) became a mark of prosperity.

Collard was the bigger name locally, although Brinsmead in Kentish Town rivalled it and boasted in 1904 that it made a

piano every hour. Collard was the older firm, having originated with the composer and musician Muzio Clementi (1752-1832) who in 1773, published what some regard as the first piece of music composed for the pianoforte. Building on his fame, Clementi formed his own piano making company in 1802 – the works in Tottenham Court Road were destroyed by fire in 1807. As from 1809 Frederick William Collard and his brother, (confusingly) William Frederick Collard were involved with the firm, called Clementi, Collard and Collard, and after Clementi's death, it became simply Collard and Collard. In

75. The fire at Collard's Oval Road factory in 1851.

76. Collard's rebuilt Rotunda in Oval Road, 2007.

1811, Frederick William patented an upright piano.

The company's new building in **Oval Road**, Camden Town, burnt to the ground in 1851, only a year after its construction. It was a well publicised fire, featuring in the *Illustrated London News*, and there was a considerable public response to raise money to replace the workmen's tools. A new building, usually called the Rotunda, was opened at the corner of Oval Road and Gloucester Crescent, which stands today. It is a generally circular building with twenty-two sections and five floors, that had a central hoist to move the pianos-to-be up and down to each department to be worked on. In the building's hinterland in Jamestown Road the company had a number of other premises that stored raw materials. The advantage that Collards had in production was that they were right next to the Regent's Canal on which the timber used was conveyed and eventually the pianos themselves were shipped. In addition, Oval Road was very near the goods depot of the London & North Western Railway. Even when the company moved in 1928, it relocated not far to Chalk Farm Road.

Modern tenants of the Rotunda have been the publishers Duckworth and Virago.

Crowndale Centre

The Centre, near the corner of Crowndale Road and Eversholt Street, houses various functions of Camden Council, in particular some of the borough's education department. Camden Town library is in part of the complex, having moved from nearly opposite the Cobden Statue in 1996. The older and main part of the building was constructed in 1912 as a principal Post Office

sorting depot for north-west London. An earlier sorting office, a few doors south, was partly supplied by the Pneumatic Despatch Railway which received mail in miniature carriages from Euston station using the pressure of compressed air in a tunnel only 4½ feet high beneath the road. This railway was opened 1863-5 and was later extended to Holborn and the City – much of the tunnel system is still used for other purposes.

In 1987-8 the building was converted into the Crowndale Centre by architects Rock Townsend.

Cumberland Basin and Market

When Regent's Park was formed in the second decade of the 19th century, the Regent's Canal was cut within it as an ornamental and commercial feature. Its function was to carry goods from the Grand Union Canal at Paddington down to the London Docks. The route taken was on the northern periphery of the Park and then, near the Zoological Gardens, went east through Camden

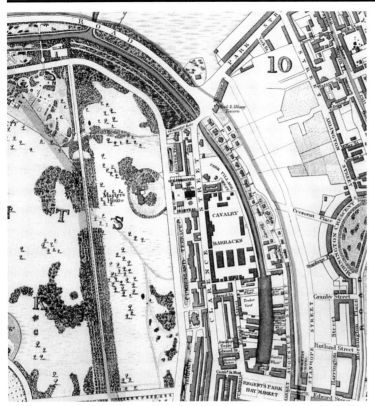

77. The stretch of the Regent's Canal down to the Cumberland Basin east of Albany Street, shown on a map of 1834. It was to here that London's Haymarket moved.

from the extension of the Piccadilly line to Cockfosters.

The open space that was left is protected by Act of Parliament and there has been much rebuilding around it since the last war.

In 1965 a model town was introduced for children but this was closed in 1986. A large renovation scheme for the young people's play area is scheduled for 2007.

Dalziel Brothers

Before the introduction of new technology in the latter part of the 19th century, most illustrations in magazines and books were obtained from wood or steel engravings. One firm stood paramount in the production of wood engravings, that of the Dalziel brothers who were born into a large family (8 sons plus daughters) from Northumberland. It was the eldest, George Dalziel (1815-1902) who set up a firm of wood engravers in London in 1839. He was joined by other brothers – Edward (1817-1905), John (1822-69) and Thomas (1823-1906) – and in 1857 the firm, known as the Camden Press and by then the best in the business, set up at 85-93 Bayham Street, in premises that extended through to an entrance at 110 Camden High Street.

The Dalziels had lucrative and prestige contracts with magazines such as *Cornhill* and *Illustrated London News*, and supplied engravings for many books including Chapman & Hall's famous illustrated edition of the work of **Dickens** – who had himself in his young days lived in the same street.

The Dalziel brothers, not content with producing the wood blocks, also commis-

Town and Islington. However, Nash devised a spur of the canal near the Zoo which ran south between Park Village East and West, past the rear of the **Albany Street** barracks and down to what became known as the Cumberland Basin. To this location, the traders who were occupying a hay market south of Piccadilly Circus (hence the street name Haymarket) were transferred so that Lower Regent Street could be constructed, thereby completing the grand highway down to the Prince Regent's Carlton House. The traders moved to Cumberland Hay Market in 1830, but it wasn't a success, even though it could be served by the canal.

Nash himself paid for much of the cost of constructing the basin. Eleven million bricks were made from the earth excavated from the site, some of which were used to build Nash's own new house in Regent Street, the **Albany Street** barracks and **Mornington Crescent**.

Also constructed on the west side of the market was a giant ice well, 82 feet deep, which, together with another one in Islington, supplied London's growing need for ice. A constant stream of ships delivered ice from Norway to Limehouse, and thence it was transported up the canal to either Gatti's ice house at New Wharf Road or the Cumberland Basin.

The market closed in 1926 and the ice well was closed in the 1930s with spoil dug up

sioned artists of the calibre of Millais, Tenniel, Leighton and Rossetti. In the 1860s and 1870s they were the most important wood engraving firm in Britain.

Their factory in Camden Town closed *c.*1905, by which time half-tone illustrations had superseded wood and steel engravings for most purposes. The family had a number of homes in Hampstead, and for a while members were at 10 Chalcot Square and 87 Albert Street.

Charles Dibdin

The life of Dibdin (1745-1814), musician, composer and performer, was one of arguments, failures, popular success and occasional financial well-being. The eighteenth son of a silver maker in Southampton, he is best remembered today as the composer of patriotic, sea-faring songs, notably *Tom Bowling*, but he began his musical career tuning harpsichords in London and then composing for that instrument. He joined Covent Garden as a chorus-singer and went on to compose pieces for productions. In 1778 he was appointed the exclusive composer for the theatre but disagreements with other members there led to him leaving. Similarly, at Drury Lane Theatre he had an argument with Garrick and left there as well. He was one of several investors in a new theatre at Blackfriars, then called the Royal Circus, but once again left after disagreements with his partners.

He fell into financial trouble, opened the Sans Souci theatre in Soho, which failed, and in later life owned a music shop, which also failed. He intended to start a new life in India,

78. *Charles Dibdin the Elder, a lithograph published in 1838.*

when an elder mariner brother, Tom, invited him to join him there. Dibdin set out, but the ship had to put in at Torbay because of bad weather and after a number of successful entertainments he gave in the area, he changed his mind and began a new career touring the country as a performer. Sadly, his brother Tom died in India and *Tom Bowling* was composed in his memory.

Eventually Dibdin, on a state pension, retired to 34 Arlington Road and upon his death was buried in **St Martin's Cemetery** (now Gardens) off Camden Street. Here was erected in 1889 a monument to his memory by the Kentish Town Musical Appreciation Society.

A descendant of Dibdin is the politician, Michael Dibdin Heseltine.

Charles Dickens

Dickens (1812-70) spent his most miserable years in Camden Town. He arrived from his school in Kent in 1822 to join his family at 16 Bayham Street (identified today as the site of 141). Into this modest house of two storeys, basement and garret were packed the parents, five children, a servant and a lodger. Dickens occupied a garret at the rear, over-

79. Charles Dickens at 18.

80. No. 141 Bayham Street (now demolished), the home of the Dickens family in 1822.

looking the backs of houses in the High Street. His father was in serious financial trouble and eventually was imprisoned for debt in Marshalsea where all his family, with the exception of Charles, joined him, as was often the case in debtors' prisons.

Charles was sent to Wellington House Academy at 247 Hampstead Road, just south of Mornington Crescent, and was boarded with a Mrs Roylance in what is now College Place. Wellington House was a conventional private school with several classes operating in a single large room. Dickens, viewing the school in 1849, wrote that the railway had by then "taken the playground, sliced the schoolroom, and pared off the corner of the house". However, **Sickert** used what was left for painting and teaching art, and though a plaque was put on the house in 1924, the building was taken down altogether in 1964 when the railway bridge was rebuilt.

In his revelations to his biographer, John Forster, Dickens painted a gloomy picture of Camden Town in the days of his childhood, although a contemporary, who had lived in Bayham Street at the same time (it was a fairly new street) leapt to the area's defence. It was, the neighbour said, like a village there. Grass struggled through the newly-paved road. There were between twenty and thirty newly-erected houses. Residents included Mr Lever, the builder of the houses, a Mr Engelhart a celebrated engraver, a Captain Blake, a retired linen draper, a retired merchant, a retired hairdresser and a Regent Street jeweller. And, as *The Streets of Camden Town* relates, other residents included the Selous family (*see* **Anti-Apartheid Movement**), and the artistic Holl family. These were hardly people who would put up with squalor. A brickfield was near, but so was haymaking. Dickens' young view was probably much coloured by his father's troubles and by his own early employment in Warren's Blacking Warehouse off the Strand, a filthy place that made shoe blacking.

In May 1824 there came an unexpected windfall on the death of his grandmother, and the family was released from Marshalsea and able to set up

81. *Wellington House Academy, Hampstead Road, the school that Dickens attended during his Camden Town days. The house, on the corner of the terrace, was eventually demolished to make way for railway and road expansion.*

house in what is now Cranleigh Street off Eversholt Street.

The Dispensary

The Dispensary movement evolved in the later 18th century to provide poor people with medical treatment cheaply or free of charge. The usual way of funding them was to invite wealthier people to pay a sum of money which would entitle them to nominate deserving cases for treatment. In Highgate, where there were numerous wealthy people, the dispensary there began in 1787 and flourished well into the 19th century, but in Camden Town, where many people were poor, fund raising relied on activities such as concerts and charitable donations. Camden Town Dispensary was in Hawley Crescent, certainly as from 1851 when it appears in the census and it was still appealing for funds in the name of a Dr Bermingham in 1889. It was usual for one or two local doc-

tors to give their services free, and any revenue from fund raising paid for overheads and medicines.

(*See also*: F Peter Woodford, 'Provident and non-provident dispensaries in Camden', *Camden History Review* 25, 2001)

Drill Halls

Volunteer fighting units emerged during the threat of Napoleonic invasion. It became the thing for local gentry to don uniforms, shoulder rifles and march in the streets, with as many of the local tradesmen and lower orders as could be mustered to follow them. After Napoleon's defeat the volunteers generally disbanded, but a new threat of French invasion in the late 1850s resulted in the setting up of volunteer rifle brigades.

The headquarters of the 19th London Regiment (previously the 17th North Middlesex Rifle Volunteers) was a drill hall at 74 Camden High

Street, opened in 1908. During the last war the hall was used for ARP training and the distribution of ration books and gas masks, while around the corner in King's Terrace, off Plender Street, was a Civil Defence and Training Centre.

Peggy Duff

Peggy Duff (1910-81) was a St Pancras and Camden councillor who achieved a national reputation for her work in the campaigns to end capital punishment and for nuclear disarmament. She first joined Sir Richard Acland's Common Wealth party during the last war, and afterwards was business manager of the left-wing magazine *Tribune*. In 1955 she became secretary of the National Campaign for the Abolition of Capital Punishment, set up that year by Sidney Silverman in response to the execution of Ruth Ellis. In 1956 she was elected as a Labour member of St Pancras council, eventually becoming its Chief Whip – she continued to be a councillor when Camden was formed.

Parliament suspended the use of capital punishment in 1965 and abolished it altogether in 1969, but by then Peggy had moved on, in 1958, to direct another and more famous cause. The Campaign for Nuclear Disarmament at its peak had hundreds of thousands of active followers. To organize it and its famous marches demanded enormous energy and inventiveness. Peggy Duff's style appeared to be rather slapdash and haphazard, but the campaign produced the largest popular demonstrations that had been seen in Britain since the war.

In 1967 Peggy resigned from the Labour Party because of

82. The headquarters of the 17th North Middlesex Rifle Volunteers was at 74-76 Camden High Street. The personalities at the opening ceremony are depicted here.

83. Peggy Duff at Aldermaston in 1961. Photo by her son, Euan Duff.

Harold Wilson's support for the USA in the Vietnam war and his refusal to condemn the Greek colonels for their takeover in Greece.

A brown Camden Council plaque marks her house at 11 Albert Street.

Edinburgh Castle

Tucked away in Mornington Terrace is a pub which once housed a museum of curiosities – the illustration on the next page depicts some of them. They were amassed in the late 19th century by its proprietor, Thomas Middlebrook, and when sold in 1908 the catalogue included the bugle which sounded the charge at the Battle of Balaklava, and a collec-

84. Advertisement for the Edinburgh Castle Free Museum.

tion of 80,000 butterflies. One of its prize exhibits was an egg of the Great Auk, a large bird which was last seen officially in 1852, but had already been extinct for some years in its natural habitat of eastern Canada, Greenland, Iceland and Norway. It had been hunted out of existence and its eggs were regarded as museum pieces.

The pub was badly damaged by fire in 1984 but restored three years later.

Electric Ballroom

At the time of writing (June 2007) the future of the Electric Ballroom at 184 Camden High Street is unclear. Transport for London have proposed several plans for redeveloping the **Camden Town Underground** site – the station is hopelessly inadequate and does need much improvement. However, TfL want to erase much of its immediate vicinity at the same time and develop with the usual offices and shops. This would mean the end of the Ballroom and a number of well established Camden institutions nearby – the present nature of this part of Camden Town would be erased in the process.

The Electric began in the 1930s as an Irish social club called the Buffalo. In 1938 it was bought by Bill Fuller, a 20-year-old contractor and former wrestler, who continued it as an Irish ballroom but improved its quality and standing with numerous showbands. He also extended the premises taking advantage of a bomb-damage site adjacent. The style of the venue changed in July 1978 when, still under his management, it became the Electric Ballroom and increasingly the entertainment was rock music in tune with the changed nature of that part of Camden High Street. Bands which have played there include the Sex Pistols, Clash, U2 and Oasis, and more recently Goth nights have been the most popular. Paul McCartney gave a memo-

85. The Electric Ballroom in Camden High Street.

rable performance there in June 2007.

As Gerry Harrison remarks in his history of the **London Irish Centre**, when comparing the present Ballroom with the Irish social club it replaced, "Now the customers ... arrive at all hours. There are still bouncers, more threatening in appearance and equipped with walkie-talkies rather than fast thinking and the gift of Irish wit, but the intentions remain the same. The music has changed. Tattoos, piercing and jeans have replaced the shiny clean faces, the white shirts, flared trousers and taffeta skirts."

Elm Village

The 'Village' was built in the 1980s on part of the old Midland Railway goods yard as a mix of private and housing association land. Its name derives from Elm Lodge, the early 19th- century home of William Agar (*see* **Agar Town**), through whose land the **Regent's Canal** runs.

Belle Elmore

Belle Elmore was an undistinguished music hall artist who sometimes performed at the **Bedford Theatre** in Camden Town. As such she would not be remembered today, but she is famous for being the wife of Dr Harvey Hawley Crippen, and for being murdered by him, resulting in his much publicised arrest, trial and execution in 1910. Belle, born in America, was the daughter of a Russian Pole and his German wife. Her original name was Kunigunde Mackamotski which she changed to Cora Turner, the name she had when she met Crippen. After marriage she

86. *Belle Elmore.*

came with him to London where he had a well paid job for an American patent medicine company and here, under the stage name of Belle Elmore, she exploited what talent she had for singing and dancing. Though not well regarded as an artist she was however Honorary Treasurer of the Music Hall Ladies Guild.

Crippen and Belle lived first in South Crescent off Tottenham Court Road, then in Store Street and lastly at 39 Hilldrop Crescent, just on the Islington side of Brecknock Road. By the time they settled at the latter house, he had only a modest salary and she, apparently, had just the income from infrequent appearances on the stage, some of them at the **Bedford Theatre**. But they lived in style, especially Belle, who revelled in dresses, furs and ostentatious jewelry. Crippen was a modest, uncommunicative man, and she was the outgoing, flirtatious one, dominant in the marriage. He, however, began an affair with his secretary, Ethel le Neve, who lived in the first St Pancras council block,

62

Goldington Buildings (now Court), at the southern end of Royal College Street. When Belle discovered this she threatened to leave, taking their joint savings with her. Facing financial ruin, and in any case in thrall to Ethel, Crippen poisoned her and buried her in the cellar of their house.

The rest of the story is the stuff of criminal history. He and Ethel (she disguised as a young man) fled to Canada on the *Montrose* liner. They were arrested by the time they reached their destination since the captain had been notified of their presence by the novelty of radio. The pair were brought back to trial in England. He was found guilty and hanged at Pentonville Prison in November, and she was found innocent in the matter.

Etcetera Theatre

This fringe theatre, one of the most successful in London, was founded by David Bidmead in 1986 above the Oxford Arms pub in Camden High Street. In 1996 it received the Guinness Ingenuity Award for Pub Theatre, and its extensive repertoire of new writing has included new plays by Ayckbourn and a rewrite of *Kafka's Dick* by neighbour **Alan Bennett**. The 2007 programme is a crowded one.

Famous names

Many well-known names are mentioned in entries throughout this book, but there are others. The earliest is the painter *George Morland* (1763-1804), who died of drink, and who had a studio at what was then 9 Warren Place in 1788 – Woolworth's in the High Street now covers the site. He was conveniently near the Mother Black

87. George Morland.

Cap pub. Other artists included *Clarkson Stanfield* (1793-1867), marine painter, who was at 1 Mornington Crescent and later next door at 263 Hampstead Road; *George Cruikshank* (1792-1878), the caricaturist and illustrator, was also at 263 Hampstead Road from 1850-78; in addition he kept a home for his mistress and many offspring around the corner in Augustus Street.

Cruikshank succeeded Gillray as the most influential artistic satirist and commentator, but he also illustrated many books including some of the publications of fellow Camden Town resident Charles Dickens. One of Cruikshank's most famous cartoons was *The March of Bricks and Mortar* (1829), which depicted the unstoppable spread of building in London's suburbs.

88. Clarkson Stanfield, marine artist.

89. George Cruikshank, the eminent caricaturist of his day.

90. Sir William Crookes.

Sir Charles Groves, the conductor (1915-92), was at 12 Camden Square at the time of his death. *Sir Eugene Goossens*, composer and conductor (1893-1962) was born in Rochester Square.

Charlotte Mew (1869-1928) was a diffident but very talented poet, whose work was admired by peers such as Virginia Woolf, Siegfried Sassoon and John Masefield. Her home from 1922-6 was at 86 Delancey Street.

Charlotte's life was plagued by misfortune. Her father, Frederick (who designed Hampstead Town Hall), died early leaving his family in poor circumstances. Two of her siblings were sent to mental institutions and another three died very young. Only Charlotte, who suffered badly from depressions, and her sister Anne survived, but always poor despite a growing reputation for Charlotte's poetry. When Anne died, Charlotte relapsed into a profound depression and in 1928 committed suicide by drinking detergent.

The novelist *Elizabeth Jane Howard* (b. 1923) moved to 28 Delancey Street on the collapse of her marriage to Kingsley Amis. She was at this address until 1990. Her best known work is a family saga which was serialized as *The Cazalets* on television. In 2002 she published her autobiography.

Sir William Crookes (1832-1919), scientist and discoverer of thallium, lived at 20 Mornington Terrace until 1881 – council flats now occupy the site.

John Desmond Bernal (1901-71) was an influential scientist specializing in crystallography but was best known to the world at large as an articulate and devoted Marxist until his death. There is a blue plaque to his residence at 46 Albert Street.

George Jacob Holyoake (1817-1906) was a founding father of the Co-operative movement and prolific writer. He lived at Dymoke Lodge in Oval Road in the 1860s.

The actor *Denholm Elliott* (1922-92) lived at 75 Albert Street in 1975, and the fashion editor of the *International Herald Tribune*, *Suzy Menkes* (b. 1943) lived in Gloucester Crescent in the 1980s. *Noel Gallagher* of Oasis lived in the basement of 83 Albert Street 1995-6. He wrote one of his best-known hits, *Wonderwall*, here.

Fleet river

When consideration was given in 1964 to the name of the new borough of Camden, at the merger of Hampstead, St Pancras and Holborn, it was suggested that it should be called Fleet. There was logic to this since the river once ran above ground through all three boroughs. The Fleet has two sources, one in the Vale of Health and the other at Kenwood. The two arms join west of Kentish Town Road, and then the river runs south to Camden Town, crossing the Kentish Town Road to the rear of Sainsbury's, and then southeast to flow between Royal College Street and St Pancras Way, through the grounds of the Veterinary College, and then roughly on the route of Pancras Road down to King's Cross. The presence of this stream might well have persuaded the founders of the **Royal Veterinary College** (which dealt mainly with horses) that they had chosen a convenient site.

The Fleet eventually disgorged into the Thames at Blackfriars and was used by all and sundry, including slaugh-

91. *The Fleet going south-east from Kentish Town Road just south of the railway bridge and near to the entrance of Sainsbury's car park. It then flows beneath a track which eventually became Royal College Street. From King's Panorama, early 19th century.*

terhouses, as a receptacle for refuse of all kinds until the southern end was covered over. Further north, at Farringdon, it kept a number of water wheels turning – hence Turnmill Street. Further north still it ran in front of Old St Pancras church and here, in rainy seasons it would flood due to silting and inadequate space so that Pancras Wash, as the area was called, became difficult to cross. This had been a problem since medieval times, serious enough for St Pancras parish to build a chapel-of-ease at Kentish Town which was easier for most people to get to. A local resident, Samuel Bagster, remembered the river *c.*1760 and said that it was "a clear ever-flowing rivulet of five or six feet wide and about a foot deep, unless when swollen by long continued rain". In 1818 the whole area between the church and today's King's Cross was flooded to 3ft deep.

Part of the river's course at Camden Town is shown in **King's Panorama** above. Here, we are at the lower end of Kentish Town Road just south of the present railway viaduct, and we are looking south-east near the Sainsbury car park entrance. The Fleet has emerged from beneath Kentish Town Road and is then, as we can see, bridged over at what became Royal College Street. It was this part of Kentish Town Road that was quite often called Water Lane, from the frequent inundations of the river – the name is perpetuated today in a small turning near the railway viaduct. Here, the Regent's Canal was constructed *above* the Fleet.

The history of this river has been described as a decline from a river to a brook, from a brook to a ditch, and from a ditch to a drain. For indeed the Fleet is now just part of the sewerage system of north London.

Gentrification

Gentrification, a word often associated with Camden Town, is a pejorative term. It implies and criticises the displacement of working class residents by middle class professionals who have the money to buy the older houses and renovate them. The process is also known as urban renewal. However described, it has been going on since the 1960s in Camden Town, slightly later than in Barnsbury in Islington which, in London, was probably the beginning.

The reasons for gentrification are many. When the last war ended much of inner London's housing stock outside of the wealthier areas was regarded as almost redundant. Borough councils implemented housing schemes which swept away streets and replaced them with estates. In St Pancras and then in Camden, much of West Kentish Town was rebuilt, as were the streets east of Albany Street to give way to the Regent's Park estate. Elsewhere in Camden Town blocks replaced sub-standard or bombed housing. It was not of interest to those councils to renovate the slum terraces that still survived – they hadn't the imagination, knowledge or skill to do so – and the surviving premises, if nothing had changed, would have been demolished in their turn. Politically, demolition and rebuilding as estates was a Utopian movement, and not just a practical one. Based on the garden city type estates that the London County Council had put up before the war, it was considered that the working classes should be rehoused in modern buildings.

Destruction and rebuilding took place over two decades, at the end of which it was recognized just how much social damage was being done and, to make matters worse, the new housing was built at a time when architecture was at its cheapest and nastiest. In contrast, the surviving terraces of modest old houses acquired some friends and more importantly for their future upkeep, some new owners.

In any case, working class tenants had gradually been moving out of Camden Town of their own accord. Furthermore, the borough councils which were building new estates were the same ones following government guidelines in persuading industry, heavy and light, into new towns where houses awaited the workers – the closure of the **Carreras** factory at Mornington Crescent is a prime local example. Additionally, the gradual removal of rent control, which itself had made it unlikely that private landlords would renovate their properties, meant that higher rents in still unmodernised properties encouraged people to look elsewhere for better housing and better value. Much of the surviving terrace housing in such streets as Arlington Road, Albert Street, the Camden Street area and Camden New Town, was multi-occupied with inadequate facilities. Streets of small houses, such as those east of Chalk Farm Road, were very overcrowded, often with no access to a bath, and usually with a shared lavatory. An excellent collection of memories put together in *Primrose Hill Remembered* and published by the Friends of Chalk Farm Library in 2001, underlines just how much of Chalk Farm was multi-occupied by working-class families before and after the last war.

As tenants moved out the private landlords, often without the capital to modernise, were happy to sell to buyers who themselves were sometimes the offspring of old London residents who had moved into suburbia in the inter-war years. The incomers appreciated the simple and harmonious architecture of London's terraces and recognized their potential; they were cheap enough to spend money on, and to take a gamble that they would eventually make a return. Furthermore, so close to London, there was no daily trek to and from the suburbs. Once the white paint appeared on the stucco outside, so others followed.

Some of the terraces were bought, often by compulsory purchase, by local councils for social housing. Camden, for example, bought the Bartholomew estate in Kentish Town and renovated it after first considering its demolition. But on the whole projects to convert and modernize old terrace housing were left to those new owners with more money than the previous ones.

The result is that we now have very expensive renovated terraces and blocks of poorly maintained social housing now that the borough has lost heart in providing it because of the 'right-to-buy' legislation. What has been missing, though much thought has been given to it, is the provision of housing for people of moderate means, who are in full employment but cannot afford to buy into Camden Town's renovated streets.

Gilbeys'

The drinks company, Gilbeys', once dominated Camden Town goods yard, occupying 20 acres and several large buildings. The **Roundhouse** was their bonded liquor store and their headquarters, designed by **Chermayeff**, was at the corner of Oval Road and Jamestown Road. An adjacent giant bottle store, built by William Hucks, is now converted into flats.

The firm began with the brothers Walter and Alfred Gilbey in 1857. The two of them had returned from the Crimean War, having been civilian clerks there, and on their elder brother's advice (he was a wine importer) they began their own business in the same trade but dealing in South African wines since they were subject then to a lower tax duty. Their success was almost immediate and they were able to take over the old building called The Pantheon in Oxford Street (the site in the

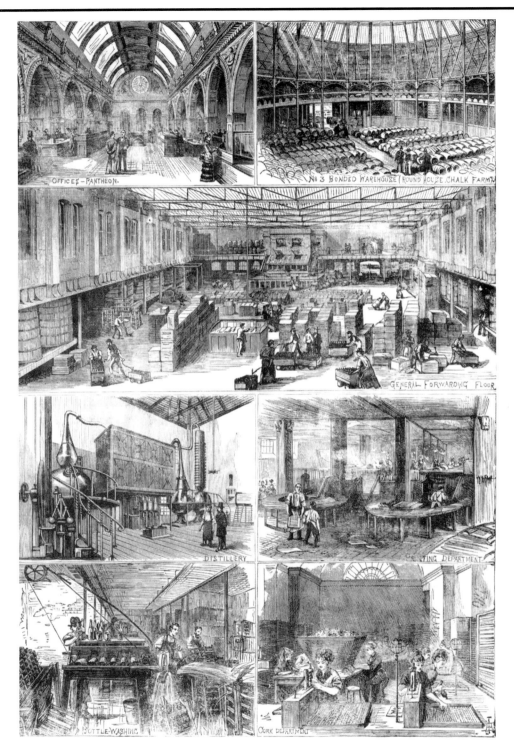

Labels within the illustration: OFFICES – PANTHEON. No 3 BONDED WAREHOUSE (ROUND HOUSE CHALK FARM). GENERAL FORWARDING FLOOR. DISTILLERY. PRINTING DEPARTMENT. BOTTLE WASHING. CORK DEPARTMENT.

92. Scenes at the various Gilbey warehouses

eastern part of the street is now occupied by a Marks and Spencer store), which had once housed fashionable concerts, balls and other entertainments.

Not only did Gilbeys' promote cheap South African wine, but they also sold single bottles – possibly the first major wine suppliers not to demand a case of twelve order. Their success was dented in 1860 when the government abandoned their high tax on French and Spanish wines and made South African wines less attractive. But at the same time off-licences were introduced and Gilbeys', always strong on promotion and advertising, used these and many agents in grocers' shops, to enlarge their business even more. By the end of that year they were the third largest wine importers in the country.

They outgrew the cavernous Pantheon and its cellars and relocated to Camden Town where they had the convenience of rail distribution at the goods yard. In 1872 they branched out into spirits, beginning a long programme of buying whisky firms and distilling their own gin – Gilbeys' gin, as a brand, became famous. By 1914 a daily train left the goods yard for the London docks containing just Gilbey products.

This seemingly unstoppable concern fell into poor financial straits after the last war and in 1962 merged with International Distillers and ten years later fell to Grand Metropolitan Hotels. The firm moved out to Harlow in 1963, leaving their many buildings in the goods yard, not to mention horse tunnels, to the developers.

Gloucester Avenue

This road, which until 1937 had three different names to its various parts, was built in the 1840s and 1850s, after the Southampton Estate was sold for development in 1840, and after the railway was constructed on its north-east side. Its name derives from the Gloucester Gate into Regent's Park. The largest building, at No. 1 facing Parkway, is now the North Bridge Senior School, an Independent Day School for children aged 11-16, which aims to place scholars in the sixth forms of better known schools in the area such as Highgate and Channing. The original house on the site was bought by nuns for a convent called Holy Rood House, but when additional tunnelling for the railway caused damage to its foundations, the house was rebuilt in its present form with a chapel attached. In the 1970s the house was taken by the Japanese School for London and then in 1987 by North Bridge School.

The houses at the Parkway end of the Avenue, on the railway side, were surprisingly lavish considering the nearness of the tracks, but it has to be remembered that at the time of their construction the railway was a modest affair and, indeed, further away from the

93. *The Holy Rood convent at the Regent's Park end of Parkway. It is now the North Bridge School.*

95. An Italianate house in Gloucester Crescent.

94. These Gloucester Avenue houses even in the 1980s still showed the pollution and neglect caused by the railway engine smoke drifting across the road.

buildings. These handsome villas – nos. 2-24 – probably by Henry Bassett, consisted of semi-detached houses and four detached villas. Their wanton demolition was permitted by a Camden Council heavily influenced by their planning director, Bruno Schlaffenberg, in 1971. They were replaced by blocks of private flats (Darwin Court) of no outward charm or merit.

Notable residents of the Avenue have included the Bassett family – the architect Henry Bassett was surveyor to the Southampton Estate – and Henry Courtney Selous the artist (no. 28, 1850s-80s) and his nephew Frederick Courtney Sealous the colonialist and big game hunter at no. 26 (*see* **Anti-Apartheid Movement**). The eldest son of Charles Dickens, also Charles, was living in the street in 1870. His *Dictionary of London* (1879) has been reissued at least once in recent years.

The status of the road deteriorated once the railway and the goods yard developed. Thick smoke drifted across the road from the maintenance depot near Dumpton Place, so much so that certainly by 1956, as this author can verify because he was living there, it was sometimes difficult to see across the street. Residents, led by local activist Stan Edmonds, protested at the pollution, at the killing of plants in gardens, at the rotting of curtains and furnishings. The Queen was petitioned in 1958. But there was no respite until electrification of the railway and the gradual closure of the goods yard.

Certainly, residents of that time would be astonished nowadays to see people happily sitting outside the Pembroke Castle pub, basking in sunshine, unaffected now by grime or smuts in their beer.

Gloucester Crescent

This road of present-day celebrities was mostly built 1845-50, though nos. 1 and 2 are slightly earlier. The style is Italianate, designed by Henry Bassett, and the street is the most prestigious in Camden Town, though many would prefer the quieter seclusion of Chalcot Crescent. Residents here have included **Alan Bennett**, artist David Gentleman, the journalist Nick Tomalin and his wife, the writer Claire Tomalin, the late George Melly and Jonathan Miller. Matthew Sturgis in his lengthy biography of **Sickert** (2004) claims that the artist also lived in the Crescent.

Goldington Court

This block of local authority flats, originally Goldington Buildings, was built 1904-5 on a plot of land which once contained the Elephant & Castle pub and a timber yard; the river Fleet flowed through the site which is at the apex of St Pancras Way and Royal College Street. It was the first St Pancras council housing and was part of a stirring start to life in the new borough – in those early years, the baths at Prince of Wales Road were opened, the Highgate branch library began, building commenced on the **Working Men's College** in Crowndale Road and the **Camden Theatre** was opened. An early resident of

96. The opening of Goldington Buildings in 1904, the first municipal housing in St Pancras.

Goldington Buildings was Ethel le Neve, secretary and mistress of Dr Crippen (*see* **Belle Elmore**).

The name of the block derives from one of the estates of the Duke of Bedford, who once owned the land.

97. Goldington Buildings soon after they were built.

The Greek community

It is estimated that between 160,000 and 220,000 Greeks live in Greater London, mostly from Cyprus, which Britain annexed in 1925. Serious immigration took place before the last war, but there was a peak, mainly due to poor living conditions on the island, from the 1950s until the mid 1960s. More followed upon the Turkish invasion of Cyprus in 1974.

Early Greek immigrants came to London in the 1670s, fleeing the Ottoman oppression in their homeland. Many settled in Soho where they erected a church on the site of St Martin's College of Art on Charing Cross Road, hence Greek Street behind it, but they abandoned it *c*.1681 as being "too remote from the abodes of most of the Grecians (dwelling chiefly in the furthermost parts of the City)".

Camden Town was a principal settlement after the last war and although the diaspora of Greek Cypriots has now largely migrated further north in London, to Haringey, Wood

70

Green, Green Lanes etc, a substantial Greek presence is still in Camden, as may be detected in the numerous Greek restaurants. It was, and is, a closely knit community, still centred around the Greek Orthodox Church of **All Saints**, appropriately a Greek Revival building by the Inwoods, which they took over from the Church of England in 1948. The community has often held large wedding receptions at such places as the forerunner of the **Electric Ballroom** and the **London Irish Centre**. The Greek Cypriot **Theatro Technis** was established in 1957.

98. *The Greenwood Almshouses in Rousden Street, 2007.*

Greenwood Almshouses

These almshouses in Rousden Street were founded in 1840 by Esther Greenwood, a niece of the then well-known entertainer Joseph Munden. A marble tablet was placed in **All Saints** church which stated that "the object of this institution is to provide an asylum, rent free, for aged women of indigent circumstances and good character – a preference being given to the inhabitants of Camden Town and Kentish Town." It was intended to house twenty such women but they were built as 12 units in four houses. The buildings were refurbished in 1985-6 as sheltered housing.

Halfway houses

The burial register for St Pancras in 1690 notes that Walter Langley was buried 'from the Halfway House'. And in 1703 a highwayman was 'shott to death' near the Halfway House and was 'buried without the service of the

Church'. Sometimes 18th-century records use the plural, 'Halfway Houses'. It is evident that the name is applied to the two alehouses, the Mother Red Cap and the Mother Black Cap, the former on the present site of the World's End in Camden Town, and the latter where the Underground station now stands. They are halfway between St Giles and Hampstead and in the seventeenth and early eighteenth centuries were virtually the only buildings of note on the road.

In 1703 a man called John Meaking, 'a chocolate maker of London' died at 'Mother Damnable's' in Kentish Town and a year later the widow who kept the 'alehouse called Mother Damnable's' died there. Mother Damnable seems to have been another name for Mother Red Cap, and emphasizes her bad repute. 'Kentish Town' was then used to include the area which is now Camden Town. The licensing records, which begin in 1721, have two Halfway Houses in 1723, and then in 1751 Mother Red Cap and Mother Black Cap

are listed under those names.

A legendary tale is printed in histories of St Pancras about Mother Red Cap – a woman called Jinney who appears to have disposed of several lovers. But as there are Mother Red Cap pubs elsewhere in the country, as far away as Bradford and as near as the Holloway Road, she is probably a rather witch-like folklore figure adopted by alehouses. Certainly she is unflatteringly depicted in a print of Mother Damnable *(ill. 101)*, 'the remarkable shrew of Kentish Town', published in 1676. The Mother Red Cap in Holloway Road (at no. 665) is mentioned in a mid 17th-century book, and indeed issued a trade token in lieu of coinage during the Restoration period. It too was sometimes called Halfway House, possibly meaning halfway between Islington and Highgate.

The ancient Mother Red Cap pub is shown in a number of prints, but most clearly in **King's Panorama** depicting the area *c.*1800. Emblazoned with the words Half Way House,

71

99. *The Mother Red Cap at the beginning of the 19th century, before the construction of Camden Road.*

100. *From a postcard depicting the 'second' Mother Red Cap, probably mid 19th century. The Camden Road is built and* **Brown's Dairy** *is on the left.*

101. *Mother Damnable, 'the remarkable shrew of Kentish Town' alleged to be the original Mother Red Cap.*

and with gardens to the left, it was host to parties retreating from London for the day. Charles Dickens remembered the sound of a band playing there during his childhood in Bayham Street, 1822-3. Much of the Red Cap's gardens disappeared when Camden Road was cut through the neighbourhood.

The pub is now part night-club and its name was changed to The World's End in 1986.

The Mother Black Cap on the Underground site was bought by St Pancras Vestry in

102. *The Mother Red Cap c.1904, by now rebuilt in its present form (The World's End).*

1775 for a **workhouse** which opened a few years later. The pub was reopened on the western side of the High Street in 1781 at today's no. 171. Now just called the Black Cap, it has been well-known for at least 25 years as a gay bar.

Oliver Heaviside

The mathematical physicist Oliver Heaviside (1850-1925) was born at 55 Plender Street. His father was a wood engraver and artist, and to make ends meet, just like Dickens' mother nearby about thirty years earlier, she opened a Dame school at their address. It was not a success and they took in lodgers instead. Heaviside recalled that "I was born and lived 13 years in a very mean street in London with the beer shop & bakers & grocers & coffee shop right opposite, & the ragged school & the sweeps just round the cor-

103. *Oliver Heaviside.*

104. The familiar Camden Town junction in the 1920s. The rebuilt Mother Red Cap is on the extreme right with what used to be called - confusingly - the Halfway House on the other side of Camden Road at the apex with Kentish Town Road. It is now called the Camden Eye. The Midland Bank, forerunner of the present bank, is in front of the Underground station. Traffic was two-way and included trams.

ner. Though born and bred up in it, I never took to it & and was very miserable there, all the more so because I was so exceedingly deaf that I couldn't go & make friends with other boys. ...The sight of the boozing in the pub made me a teetotaller for life. Well at 13, some help came, & we moved to a private house in a private street. It was like heaven in comparison, & I began to live at once..."

The new abode was 123 Camden Street, where the family stayed until 1876 and then moved on to 3 St Augustine's Road. During this period Heaviside worked in the telegraphic industry but went on to become a reclusive theoretical physicist who made extraordinary advances in the realm of telegraphic and electromagnetic science. Heaviside promoted a theory, later proved, that explained why wireless waves circled the earth instead of disappearing into space. He proposed that there must be an ionosphere which prevented this – originally called the Heaviside Layer.

For his scientific work he was made a Fellow of the Royal Society in 1891. Also, two craters, one on the moon and the other on Mars, have been named for him.

He eventually moved to Devon where he became even more reclusive and, indeed, eccentric. He moved granite blocks into his house to serve as furniture, and despite being generally unkempt, neighbours described him as having elegant painted pink fingernails.

(See David Sealey, "Low Neighbours and bad drains", *Camden History Review* 20, 1996)

105. The Hopkinson building in Fitzroy Road.

Hopkinson's piano factory

Converted now into apartments and a community centre, Hopkinson's piano factory and its ancillary building at 44 Fitzroy Road were built in 1867. Jacquetta Hawkes, who lived at 39, described the main building as 'subdued Roman' in style.

John Hopkinson began as a music publisher in Leeds in 1835, but did not establish his piano manufacturing business in London until 1846, though he always put 'Est. in 1835' on his instruments. He had several shops in the West End – at Regent Street, Conduit Street, Hanover Street and New Bond Street as well as the Brompton Road. Hopkinson retired in 1869 and died in 1886.

After Hopkinson's vacated the factory it was used to manufacture electric light fittings. Derelict for some years and threatened with demolition, it was saved by a spirited campaign by local residents in the 1980s and was handsomely converted.

Horse tunnels

Hundreds of horses were used in the Camden Goods Yard to haul wagons and goods, but as the railway was enlarged many of the animals were injured or killed as they crossed rails on their way to and from their stables. An underground tunnel was therefore built in 1854-6, parallel to Chalk Farm Road. Soon afterwards Pickford's moved their horses' stables to the site of today's Waterside Place off Gloucester Avenue and a second horse tunnel was constructed beneath the main line for them. Additionally, the towpath of the Regent's Canal was connected to the tunnels which themselves were joined at basement level in a goods shed.

One tunnel begins in today's Stables Market. It emerges at

ground level at 30 Oval Road, a building which was once the headquarters of Jim Henson's Muppet Studios.

Despite having listed building protection there have been a number of recent inroads into the tunnel system. The tunnels are earmarked to be part of the Camden Railway Heritage Trail and it would be a great pity if they are inaccessible or rendered meaningless by development.

Ice Wells

In the nineteenth century, with the burgeoning of shops and restaurants, the demand for ice grew substantially. Ice wells were not a new invention – they featured in grand estates, and even at a mansion in Highgate – and were common in the eighteenth century. Ice was gathered during winter from ponds and lakes and stored in brick built wells with domed roofs and drainage to take away water, working in much the same way as a vacuum flask by excluding warmth. But supplies to commercial establishments were quite often polluted and, indeed, dangerous to use.

As from the 1820s purer ice from Norway was brought over in great quantity. In Camden a business was set up by William Leftwich at the **Cumberland Basin**, where an ice well 82 feet deep was constructed. Ice was ferried up the Regent's Canal from the docks and stored there. Leftwich then built two ice wells between Jamestown Road and the Canal in the 1830s and was the predominant supplier for London, until Carlo Gatti, the entrepreneur and restaurateur, began as from 1857 to supply ice from his well in New Wharf Road in King's Cross – his premises now house the London Canal Museum.

The wells that once belonged to Leftwich in Jamestown Road were capped over with reinforced concrete in 1912. In November 1995, with development plans afoot, the larger of the two wells was opened up and an abseiler climbed down to see how deep it was.

Jack Whitehead, in his book on Camden Town, describes the strenuous labours of the men who removed the ice from the wells for sale to restaurants, businesses and homes:

"The ice men descended into the well in the early mornings by a steel ladder and spent up to two hours winching up the ice blocks. These could weigh from 2 to 4 hundredweight and might have to be lifted fifty feet or more." Then the blocks had to be split with ice picks into sizes that could be sold. These were then wrapped in sacking and hawked round the streets.

Thomas Howell Idris

The name Idris was once synonymous with mineral waters. In the 1950s an advertising campaign, which now probably wouldn't be pursued, depicted a black man exclaiming that he drank "Idris when I's dri".

Thomas Howell Williams (1842-1925) began to manufacture mineral water, particularly ginger beer, in 1873. Twenty years later he changed his surname to Idris, after the Cader Idris mountain in his native Snowdonia. However, he did not obtain his water from the many streams in that region, but from an artesian well in Pratt Street, Camden Town.

106. Thomas Howell Idris.

Idris lived there at no. 110, and the factory was on the east side of Royal College Street.

Idris became prominent in politics. During the Liberal heyday at the beginning of the twentieth century, he was MP for Flint in Wales from 1906-10, a St Pancras alderman, and mayor of the borough in 1903-4. He was also a St Pancras representative on the first London County Council in 1889. His son and daughter-in-law followed him as St Pancras councillors. Later, Idris lived at 14 Highgate West Hill, a house that was afterwards taken by another well-known name, the wallpaper manufacturer, William Shand-Kydd.

The Idris firm was bought by Britvic in 1987, and its products, mainly ginger beer and cream soda, are still sold.

Interchange Building

The Interchange Building on the north side of Camden Lock was built about the first years of the twentieth century to provide under one roof an interchange of goods between canal, railway and road. Above the interchange area there were three floors of storage. Nowadays the building is used for offices mainly by media companies, and the hole in the floor which used to allow a hoist to go up and down to the various levels of transport has now been filled on each level with glass tiles. Also since conversion, the railway floor, which used to be open to the elements, has been walled in. As Jack Whitehead points out in his book on the area, there are no locks on the canal between Uxbridge and Camden Town and as a result water flows very slowly until the lock is operated at Camden Town. Thus the area around the Interchange Building became silted with rubbish and detritus and its dock became known as Dead Dog Hole.

Jenny Wren and Jason

As commercial traffic on the Regent's Canal diminished almost to nothing as from the 1950s, only enthusiasts saw the value of this stretch of water and how it could be an asset instead of a rubbish-strewn liability. At Camden Lock its nature was threatened in the 1960s by the proposed **Motorway Box**, a grandiose and insensitive road scheme that would have ruined Camden Town and large parts of Hampstead. But before that, in 1951, John James began a canal cruise on a narrowboat called *Jason*, based at Little Venice. This went through picturesque Regent's Park and the Zoo and terminated at Camden Lock. And then in 1968, even before the motorway scheme was abandoned, Paddy Walker, formerly an art student and teacher at the **Working Men's College**, and more latterly an

antique dealer in Camden High Street, introduced the *Jenny Wren*, operating from Walker's Quay on the east side of the High Street at the canalside: the inveterate canal campaigner, Sir Alan Herbert, inaugurated the service. Walker also helped Viscount St Davids set up the nearby **Pirate Castle**. The *Jenny Wren* also plied the canal up to Little Venice, but later, when Inland Waterways were persuaded to improve the canal, it was possible to pleasure cruise in the opposite direction to Limehouse.

Walker died in 1998. His premises at 250 Camden High Street have in recent years been converted into a pleasant waterside restaurant.

Jewish Museum

The Jewish Museum moved from Upper Woburn Place to 129-131 Albert Street in 1995. A second centre is located in Finchley. In Camden Town the museum contains the world's finest collection of Jewish ceremonial art, but it also illustrates the settlement of Jews in this country.

Jews' Free School

The school left its Camden Road buildings in 2002 and is in new premises in Kenton. The site of its old building is now covered with houses built in the style of the neighbourhood.

The school began in 1732 in Ebenezer Square, Whitechapel as the Talmud Torah of the Great Synagogue of London, mainly serving orphans. It moved to larger premises in Bell Lane nearby and during the mass immigration of Jews fleeing pogroms in the nineteenth century the school roll sometimes reached 4000 – it was

said to be the largest school in Europe. Their building in Whitechapel was destroyed by bombing in the last war and the school was relocated in 1958 to the junction of Camden Road and Torriano Avenue.

Alumni have included Bud Flanagan, the band leader Joe Loss, the entertainer Alfred Marks, the singer Issy Bonn, the actor David Kossoff and the artist Mark Gertler.

King's Panorama

The *Panorama of Kentish Town* is almost without comparison in London historical views. Modest and grand buildings, domestic, public and agricultural, are all shown in pen and wash on both sides of the principal roads of the area, stretching from Swains Lane at the foot of Highgate West Hill, down to Old St Pancras Church and, on a spur, to Camden Town. It purports to show the roads as they appeared at the beginning of the 19th century. The artist, James Frederick King, was born in 1781, and his family home was a largish house next to the Castle Tavern in Kentish Town Road. He was a pupil at Gordon House Academy in Highgate Road in 1788 and he was there when, dramatically, the headmaster died of apoplexy in a classroom.

After marriage King lived at 3 Montague Place, on the site of what used to be the British Rail booking office next to Kentish Town Underground station – now fronted by an ornate structure which used to be part of Elstree station. From his front parlour in those rural days he would have had clear views to Parliament Hill and Hampstead. We know little of his working life, though he recorded in the 1851 census that he was a 'retired artist'. He died in 1855 of bronchitis, and is buried in Highgate Cemetery.

Though the ostensible date for his *Panorama* is *c*.1800, on examination of the watermarks of the paper it seems that the final form was drawn in 1848, possibly from memory, or more likely compiled from previous drawings made on different bits of paper at different times in his life. When compared with Thompson's very detailed parish map of *c*.1800, it is remarkably accurate, though there are discrepancies.

The *Panorama* was offered to St Pancras Council in 1930 by his granddaughter, for £36 at the prosaic rate of £1 per foot; eventually the parsimonious council got the lot for £32.8s. It then consisted of two rolls. The following year the vendor offered another, shorter roll for £15, which was also bought.

Now, the Panorama consists of three rolls, one of 20ft 7", another of 15ft 5" and the third of 3ft, a total of 38ft. The short roll shows the east side of Kentish Town Road from opposite the Castle Tavern down to the Mother Red Cap (now the World's End) in Camden Town, and one of the long rolls depicts the west side of Kentish Town Road from today's Camden Town Underground up to the area of Swains Lane. Camden High Street is not depicted.

A facsimile reproduction of this remarkable document is available either from Camden Local Studies and Archives at Holborn Library, or else from the London Topographical Society, who are its publishers. Sections of the Panorama are reproduced in illustrations 3, 91, 99 and 185.

107. *The King's Road Forge in St Pancras Way before its demolition.*

King's Road Forge

In the 1980s, shabby premises at the junction of St Pancras Way and Agar Grove proclaimed the faded painted title 'King's Road Forge'. This drew attention to the ancient name of the road – dating from the time when most main roads belonged to the Crown, though maintained by local parishes. This particular 'King's Road' led from King's Cross up Pancras Road, St Pancras Way and Kentish Town to Highgate. The name was changed to avoid confusion with other King's Roads in 1937, which, presumably tells us when the premises, at the latest, were previously painted. The Forge, of course, would have dealt with horses, but in its latter days it did odd bits of car repair.

Louis (Lajos) Kossuth

Kossuth (1802-94) was famous throughout Europe as a revolutionary leader, and in particular an advocate of independence for Hungary from the Austrian government. He was theatrical, but compelling in

108. *Louis Kossuth.*

his speeches; he was uncompromising in his aims, but lauded because of this. He endured a harsh three-year regime in prison for his views. After exile in Turkey under British protection, he was feted enthusiastically in Britain in October 1851 and received the same response when touring America. He came back to England for eight years. During that time he lived in Gower Street and then in 1861 at 12 Regent's Park Terrace in Camden Town.

Lavatories

Public lavatories for women were a rarity until the twentieth century. There were plenty of urinals for men, and in any case pubs provided them. But it was thought indelicate for women to use a public toilet. St Pancras Vestry was told in 1874 that several doctors had testified that the lack of lavatories for women had often resulted in fatal consequences. The next year a public company proposed to the vestry that they would erect and run 'retiring rooms' for women and free conveniences for poor women. Nothing came of this but in 1878 the Ladies' Sanitary Association urged action and in 1880 a Mr Alfred Watkyns applied to the vestry for leave to erect public conveniences for both sexes, styled *'chalets de toilette et de nécessité'*. They were to be 20ft long, 12ft wide and 10ft high, made of iron and wood, together with illuminated advertisements. They were to be in the charge of a female janitor, and a shoeblack would be able to trade outside of them. Watkyns' first proposed site was at the end of Parkway facing the junction with Gloucester Avenue. However, local inhabitants protested. Apart from anything else, they said, if the chalet were a pecuniary success it would "have a tendency to diminish that innate sense of modesty so much admired in our countrywomen." It was not until 1883 that Watkyns was able to erect a chalet at the junction of High Street and Parkway, the site of the present ladies' convenience.

The campaign for women's lavatories was championed by George Bernard Shaw who was a St Pancras vestryman and a borough councillor when the borough was established.

Lawford's

The Lawford building supplies firm was once a landmark by the side of the canal opposite Lyme Terrace – their site, once known as College Wharf and Devonshire Wharf, is now taken by new development and the firm's administration is in Finchley. John Eeles Lawford established a business as a slate merchant in the Euston Road in 1840; a few years later he took the site by the canal in Camden Town. It was his son, John Eeles jnr who expanded the firm into Willesden, Edgware, Finchley and Highgate. He also branched out into house building, responsible for much of Lawford, Woodsome and Laurier Roads in Kentish Town. John Eeles the younger was also a long-serving St Pancras vestryman and churchwarden.

109. A Lawford foreman, horse and cart at the Camden Town wharf in 1923.

110. The Lawford Wharf from Lyme Terrace, drawn by G H Cook in 1925.

Leverton's

Leverton's, the firm of undertakers at the northern end of Eversholt Street, are undoubtedly the oldest ratepayers in Camden. In 1789, when coffin makers also 'undertook' to perform other services for the bereaved, including carpentry, John Leverton set up business in Henry Street off the west side of Hampstead Road, a road now demolished. He died in 1843 and was interred in the burial ground of St James's Chapel, Hampstead Road. When that burial ground was closed and turned into a secluded garden some tombstones, including that of Leverton, were stacked around the perimeter. His was found by Basil Leverton, then a senior partner, in the 1960s and it was recut and replaced in the garden.

Leverton's set up their main office in Eversholt Street on a site now occupied by the **Crowndale Centre**, but moved later a few doors south to no. 212.

The firm descended through subsequent generations of Levertons, becoming larger through the years with branches in a number of places in north London.

Ivor Leverton (1914-2005) was involved during the last war in an elaborate plot to fool the Germans, which involved using a body which Leverton's had in their care. This was done with the encouragement of the coroner and the permission of the family involved. The tale is told in the film *The Man who never was*, made in 1956.

The firm has remained independent against a background of many undertakers being taken over by conglomerates. It was partly this independence that led to the firm being chosen about twelve years ago by the Royal Family to supervise its funerals. And it was Leverton's who arranged the spectacular funerals of Diana, Princess of Wales and of Queen Elizabeth the Queen Mother. The Daimler hearse that carried them both was put up for sale in 2003 for £100,000.

Libraries

St Pancras Vestry and its successor, St Pancras Borough, were slow off the mark in providing public libraries. Though legislation in 1850 made them possible, it was not until 1906 that St Pancras Council, with the Progressives (a mix of Liberals and left-wing councillors) in control, opened their first purpose built library – on a free site in Highgate New Town, out of reach of most of the population. The next branch was a 'temporary' one at 18 Camden Street, in premises once occu-

111. The funeral cortège of Henry Croft, King of the Pearly Kings, in 1930, led by Stanley Leverton. The procession is leaving the southern end of Eversholt Street, turning into Euston Road. The four horses pulling the hearse wear velvets, which will be removed before they begin to trot. Members of the Pearly fraternity walk beside the hearse.

pied by Miss Buss and her North London Collegiate School. This was not replaced until 1964, when in a concentrated burst of library building in the 1960s, a branch was established at 12 Camden High Street, an address that had had two notable previous occupants – the **North London Collegiate School for Boys**, and **Oetzmann's** the cabinet maker. The library moved once more in 1996, to be accommodated in the **Crowndale Centre**.

Another temporary branch opened in a former confectioner's at 109 Regent's Park Road in 1947. It had a very small stock and readers were allowed just two tickets, and only one of these could be for fiction. This was replaced in 1961 by a new branch in Sharpleshall Street. Threatened with closure, a campaign by local residents saved the building in 1998.

Sir Oliver Lodge

Two eminent physicists have been associated with Camden Town. One is **Oliver Heaviside**, the other, Oliver Lodge (1851-1940). Born in Stoke-on-Trent, Lodge first came to London as a youth when he stayed with his aunt in Fitzroy Square. It was on this visit that he took his first interest in the sciences and later he returned to stay with his aunt (this time she was in Burton Crescent) to take courses at the South Kensington Museum. In 1874 he went to University College to study and took lodgings at 62 Delancey Street, Camden Town. He recalled in his memoirs: "I had to practise the strictest economy, and preferred to buy my own bread and cheese and occasional cooked meat, which I used to carry home in a newspaper and keep until it

112. *A bust of Oliver Lodge.*

was all consumed leaving no scraps … Horse tramcars were then running from Camden Town to Tottenham Court Road, but I very seldom allowed myself to do anything but walk. Every penny was of value…"

He was at Delancey Street for three years, until his marriage. After the honeymoon they went to new lodgings at Harrington Square opposite Mornington Crescent, "but the landlady was appalled at the amount of luggage" and refused to take them in. "Ultimately, we settled down in the Camden Road. Thence we migrated to Kentish Town."

Lodge specialized in the study of the ether and wireless. He made a demonstration of radio waves at the annual meeting of the British Association for the Advancement of Science, in 1894 – this was two years before Marconi's first broadcast. Lodge also made a major contribution to motoring by inventing the electric spark ignition for the internal combustion engine. He became a Fellow of the Royal Society in 1887, and in 1900 he accepted an offer to become the first Principal of Birmingham University.

He wrote a number of works proposing that there was survival after death and in this was a supporter of Sir Arthur Conan Doyle (*see* **Spiritualists**). He was not, in the usual sense, a Spiritualist, but he was convinced of the ability of mediums to connect with a world apart from physical reality.

The London Irish Centre

The Irish have been a significant proportion of Camden Town's population for over a hundred and fifty years. They first arrived in force as workers when the main railway lines to Euston, King's Cross and St Pancras were constructed (1834-68). And when the substandard houses of Somers Town that many of them lived in were themselves swept away for railway expansion, the Irish moved further north to Camden and Kentish Towns. This fevered railway construction coincided with the peak of the Irish potato famine in 1847, and men, desperate for work came to London.

The next large waves of immigrants occurred in the later 1940s and 1950s lured by jobs in the burgeoning construction industry after the war. Their strength and their skills were in demand, if poorly paid, but the available accommodation for them was wretched. Gerry Harrison in his book on the London Irish Centre (*see below*) gives a graphic picture of their difficult lives. Most of them were employed on a daily basis, just as the dock workers in east London were, and bad weather meant, possibly, no employment. They had tiring, muddy days, and evenings in which they were not welcome to stay

113. Tom McNamara, one of the founders of the London Irish Centre, outside the hostel with early arrivals.

at their lodgings unless it was to sleep. So, a great deal of their time and money was spent in Irish pubs. It was a lonely life, away from the intimacies of their family in Ireland. Harrison describes how each morning, from six, they congregated at certain parts of Camden Town, such as Peter's Café in Camden Road, waiting to be picked up and employed by the medium-sized contractors such as Lowery's or Murphy's (there were two Murphy firms, run by brothers).

The Catholic church in the area worried that the Irish workers were drifting away from religion because of their social plight and the lack of a family to reinforce their religious observance.

It was partly this concern that brought about the foundation of the London Irish Centre by two priests, Tom McNamara

and Ambrose Woods. They raised the money to buy 52 Camden Square for £3887 in August 1955. It was a large property formerly occupied by a home for young offenders, and then for unmarried women and their children. Very soon afterwards next door no. 51 was bought for £2740. These properties were converted into a hostel for Irish men until they could become established both with work and lodgings.

At that time the main alternative for Irish workers of this kind was **Arlington House** in Camden Town. Harrison quotes Catherine Sullivan, who worked at the London Irish Centre, that 'Arlington House is the working man's hotel and there are 5 of these in London each run by a private company, but Arlington is the biggest. It takes 1068 men a night, 800 of whom are regulars. 35% of the

men staying there are Irish."

Always expanding, always short of money and unable to persuade the Irish government in the earlier years to give it a grant, the Centre became not just a hostel, but a social venue, an advice bureau and a lettings and employment agency. Much of this work was done by volunteers. There was a dark period at the height of the Troubles in Northern Ireland during the 1980s when the Centre was a focus for police attention.

The premises extend round to Murray Street where there is a plain building, known as Oliver Plunket House. (See Gerry Harrison *The Scattering. A History of the London Irish Centre, 1954-2004*, 2004)

London and North Western Railway

The London & Birmingham Railway was the first to enter north London. It had been mooted in 1823, and it received the support of Birmingham businesses which at that time sent a thousand tons of goods each week by canal to London; small traffic went by coach and by 1830 there were 22 coaches to the capital taking an average of 12 hours for the journey. Birmingham cast envious eyes at the success of the Liverpool and Manchester Railway, opened in 1830. In 1833 Robert Stephenson was appointed chief engineer for a 112-mile line between Birmingham and London. Taking 20,000 men nearly five years to build, it was opened in stages and was not completed until September 1838.

At first the line went only as far as Chalk Farm to the north of the Camden goods yard. Ideally, the company wanted to build their line to Euston Grove

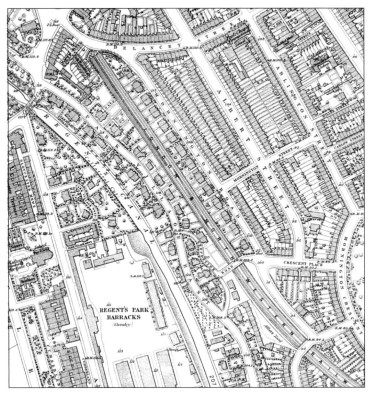

on the New Road (today's Euston Road), but there were difficulties with the landowners and there was also the problem of the incline between Camden Town and Euston – it was steeper than locomotives of the day could manage, a factor made worse by having to take the line above the Regent's Canal and beneath Hampstead Road. When the line was extended to Euston a stationary engine was installed at Camden Town to haul trains, by cable, up from Euston. Its two chimneys, shown on the cover of this book and on ill. 60, became a tourist attraction.

The line was opened from Euston to Boxmoor on 20 July 1837 and the whole line on 17 September 1838. The station at Euston was a temporary one,

114. An 1870s map of the L & NWR route through the lower part of Camden Town.

115. A train entering an engine shed at Camden in 1839.

116. Constructing the line in the 1830s.

117. The railway looking south from Parkway, depicted in 1837 by R B Schnebbelie. The church in the centre is New St Pancras Church on Euston Road. There is still a view, looking over the wall from the end of Parkway, but it is now more obscured.

118. *Some Marine Ices products.*

119. *Krishna Menon.*

and the subsequent grandiose classical structure, designed by Philip Hardwick and his son Philip Charles Hardwick (demolished 1962) was opened in stages – the Great Hall was not completed until 1849.

In 1846 the London & Birmingham merged with the Grand Junction Railway and a few other companies to form the London & North Western Railway, which in turn was later absorbed into the London Midland and Scottish Railway. It was nationalized in 1948 and is now part of the privatized West Coast Main Line.

The railway's effect on Camden Town has been immense. Had it not been built the whole area north of the canal would surely have been developed for housing.

Marine Ices

Marine Ices at 8 Haverstock Hill is a Camden Town institution, renowned for its ice creams and sorbets. Its story begins in 1900 when Gaetano Mansi, aged 12, was sent over from Ravello in southern Italy to live with relatives, in the hope that there would be a bet-

ter future for him in England. Those relations made ice cream in Bermondsey and in 1908 Gaetano opened his own business in Drummond Street, near Euston station, and then another in Euston Road itself.

The Haverstock Hill ice cream parlour began in 1930 and the Mansi family have continued to run the business since.

In 1947 the shop was rebuilt by Aldo Mansi, Gaetano's eldest son, when it became known as Marine Ices. This building was somewhat in the shape of the bridge of a ship with a 'porthole' that can still be seen in

the centre of the present ice cream parlour. In 1984 a restaurant was added.

Krishna Menon

Menon (1897-1974) was born into an affluent family in Calicut, Kerala, southern India. While in college he began to take an interest in the movement which sought independence of Britain. He also became involved in Theosophy and met its guru, Annie Besant, who was also an enthusiast for Home Rule for India - she helped him to travel to England in 1924 to further his studies.

In London he attended University College and the London School of Economics, and continued his support for Indian independence.

1934 was a fruitful year for him: he was called to the Bar, obtained his M.Sc and was elected to St Pancras borough council for Ward 4 (Chalk Farm ward). He was involved in a number of St Pancras committees, notably the Education and Libraries Committee in 1945. It was Menon who was chairman when the St Pancras Arts and Civic Council was established in 1946 – the forerunner of the famed St Pancras Arts Festival. Before he left for India he worked as an editor for Pelican Books and the Twentieth Century Library.

In his St Pancras years Menon lived at 7 Camden Terrace, Camden Square. Unfortunately, his residence has been misinterpreted because Camden Council erected a plaque to his memory on 57 Camden Square instead.

Menon, though a member of the Labour Party, was very much to its left. He was an activist in the Indian Independence movement, so much so that he was of interest to MI5 before and after the war. He was an articulate and persuasive speaker, but sometimes wearisome, such as the occasion he spoke for five hours at the United Nations on the subject of Kashmir.

He returned to India in 1947 when India was granted independence. He was much favoured by Nehru, but unpopular amongst many in the Congress Party. Nehru planted him as the member of Parliament for Bombay – an outsider, in effect – an intrusion that led to him being dropped once Nehru had gone.

Described by many as rude, arrogant and sarcastic, he also took the blame when as Defence Minister, India was humbled in the Indo-Sino conflict of 1962.

Methodists

The Methodist footprint on Camden Town has been light. Wesleyan Methodists had a small chapel in Kings Terrace, behind today's Camden Town Methodist church in Plender Street. They sold this and built another chapel off Camden Street in 1860, on a site subsequently used for the new hall built by Camden Council to accompany the new **Artists' Studios**. The chapel was used for the manufacture of barrage balloons during the last war.

The Primitive Methodists built what is usually called the Camden Town Methodist Church in Plender Street in 1889. Seating 600, it was designed by T & W Stone.

Midland Railway

The Midland Railway came late into London. It originated as a minor line in the 1830s, its main function the conveyance of coal mined in the Midlands. In 1844 a number of Midland railway companies merged to form the Midland Railway. The most important market for their freight, particularly coal, was London, but other than an arrangement with the London & North Western Railway to use its lines, they had no way of getting goods to the capital. An improvement came in 1857 when the Midland built a line

120. *The Midland Railway showing its route through part of Kentish Town, beneath Camden Road and Camden Square, and out beyond Agar Grove.*

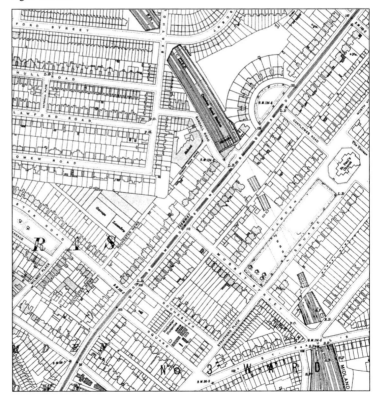

121. *The Camden Road station of the Midland Railway, at the junction with Sandall Road c.1904. The North London Collegiate School for Girls is on the left. The station, closed in 1916, was until recently supplanted by a petrol station, but this is now a car wash.*

to Hitchin and from there shared the lines of the Great Northern into King's Cross. But the relationship deteriorated, especially as the Great Northern's traffic increased and the GNR gave priority to its own trains, both passenger and freight.

The remedy, of course, was for the Midland to open its own terminus. But where? King's Cross and Euston stations were already located on the Euston Road, and the line had to terminate at that highway, since the government had forbidden train companies to the north of London to cross it. But by the time the Midland came to build its terminus much of the land north of Euston Road was built upon, and any new line would have meant the destruction of considerable property. Furthermore, the line, just like the GNR and the L&NWR would have to cross the Regent's Canal one way or another.

Against strong opposition from competitors the Midland won parliamentary assent in 1863 to construct a line from Bedford to Euston Road to where St Pancras Station now stands, with additional land bought from Lord Somers nearby. This meant the destruction of seven slum streets and the eviction of about 3,000 people without compensation or provision of alternative accommodation. It also caused much destruction and interference in the two burial grounds by St Pancras Old Church – the removal of the dead provoked much more uproar than the eviction of the living. St Pancras Station, or at least the shell of it, opened on 1 October 1868, though goods traffic had already been sent through to a station near Agar Grove in September 1867.

The line crossed Kentish Town and Camden New Town, but in the event was relatively unobtrusive, though south of

Agar Grove the whole area became, together with the Great Northern property, 'railway lands', where trains were serviced and goods dealt with.

The Midland line had a station at Kentish Town and from there burrowed through the Caversham estate to Sandall Road where there was a station (*see above*) – this closed in 1916 as a wartime economy, though it had been poorly used because of the competition of tramways. The line crossed beneath Camden Road here – its path is marked today by two petrol station buildings facing each other, for it was not possible to build anything much heavier on what is essentially a railway bridge. Then the railway goes at a sub level through Camden Square, Murray Mews and the junction of St Augustine's Road and Murray Street down to St Pancras – a route easy to track at ground level.

122. *The Mormon Chapel in Royal College Street.*

Mormons

After a history in the United States as schismatic as that of the Methodists or Baptists in England, the Mormons moved into the Salt Lake, Utah area in 1847. In 1849 the following newspaper cutting appeared in a Camden Town paper:

"This sect is rapidly increasing in numbers in the neighbourhood of Camden and Somers Towns and intend in the spring of the year to emigrate and colonise in California. They have arranged to hire the use of four or five vessels for their own conveyance to the Western World. On their arrival in California, they intend to pursue their route to the 'Valley of the Salt-water Lake', enter upon farms, and encourage agriculture. They 'hold' all things common among themselves, and are strictly bound by the ties of fraternization and socialism."

Camden History Society's *Streets of Camden Town* has identified a meeting place for Camden Town Mormons at nos. 87-89 Royal College Street, from 1854 to 1858. In that year the group disbanded and merged with the Somers Town branch for some years before reforming in 1870 briefly at 50 Camden High Street.

Mornington Crescent and its Station

The Crescent has seen better days. When built in the 1820s it was an elegant grouping, with a view to Park Village and Regent's Park to the rear, and private gardens at the front. The houses were occupied mainly by professional people – the eminent artist, Clarkson Stanfield, lived at no.1 (then numbered 36) in 1832. But then came the first intrusion, the London & Birmingham (later London & North Western) Railway, whose line was extended down to Euston in 1837, came in at the rear of the Crescent to pass beneath Hampstead Road. As the frequency of service and the capability of locomotives increased so did the amount of smoke and dirt they emitted, and gradually the Crescent suffered, just as the rest of Camden Town did, a conversion into multi-occupation and lodging houses.

The Crescent, named after the Earl of Mornington, Governor-General of India, elder brother of the Duke of Wellington, and friend of the landowning Fitzroy family, was already in a bad way when the building of the **Carreras factory** on the gardens in 1926 took away any cachet it still retained. From henceforth the residents, still with a smattering of professional residents, such as a physician, dentist and a solicitor, looked out at the rear of a

123. Mornington Crescent c.1950.

factory from their front windows, and railway land behind. But at least the furore that accompanied the sale of the gardens and the subsequent factory building led to the formation of the Royal Commission on London Squares whose remit was to prevent such development happening again.

Notable occupants of the Crescent have included **Walter Sickert** at no. 6, and fellow Camden Group artist Spencer Frederick Gore (1874-1914) at 31. Other residents at no. 1 have been architect Edward Paraire, here from 1866 to 1882 – he designed the Club Room at Lord's Cricket Ground – and the prolific composer Wilfred Josephs (1927-97), who lived with his family in Flat 1. He was frequently featured in the annual St Pancras and then Camden Arts Festival.

At no. 36 (then numbered 1) there was an Institution for the Sons of Missionaries from 1852 until 1857.

The Underground station was opened on what became the **Northern Line** in 1907, but only for the Edgware branch

trains. It was closed *c.*1992 because its lifts had become inoperable and there were many rumours that it would be closed altogether, leaving a large section of population between Warren Street and Camden Town without a tube stop. However, it was refurbished and reopened in 1998 with a ceremony featuring the famed cast of the BBC's *I'm Sorry I Haven't a Clue*, whose frequent playing of the Mornington Crescent game has made the station famous. The rules of the game have long since disappeared from common memory, even if they were there in the first place, and the team seemingly make them up each time to everyone's delight. There are innumerable websites devoted to the game, but the most likely version of the rules explains, confusingly: "When the game was first played it was based on the 1952 A-Z and a simple formula dictating to which pages one could move and to which pages one could not move. The art of the game was to make a move that made it impossible to move to one of the

pages on which Morn-ington Crescent appeared on the next move or in three moves time, or even in five moves time..."

The Motorway Box

'The Motorway Box' was shorthand for one of the most damaging proposals emanating at first from the London County Council and then its successor the Greater London Council. There were early suggestions in the later 1950s and then a full-blown scheme was published in 1966.

The plan was for three 8 or 6-lane ringways (it was never quite clear which) connected to the new motorways such as the M1 and M4, to feed traffic away from the centre of London if it was destined for another side of the city. Ringway 1 was the scheme that affected Hampstead and Camden Town as well as Islington. It began at Willesden where it had links to the M1, and was to be built over the North London Line, entering Hampstead at Maresfield Gardens, then went through Fitzjohns Avenue, Belsize Park and Eton Avenue to emerge on the slopes of Primrose Hill, all by cut and cover. At Adelaide Road, where the new road would be at elevated level, it would just miss the Round House, carry on over railway land and there connect with a feeder road near Camden Lock which would continue south along one side of Oval Road, down to Mornington Terrace and Crescent and then disgorge traffic to the centre of town. Meanwhile, the main ringway would continue east into Islington and there would be another feeder road above Camden Road which would cross Camden High Street and Camden Street down to Hampstead Road. It was estimated that 2250 houses would have to be demolished to make way for this mess. There was no estimate as to how much misery it would cause nearby residents whose remaining properties would hear the noise and receive the fumes.

As regards the cut-and-cover sections, the idea was, said a GLC engineer, that once the motorway had been built the environment could be "replaced over the top. Houses can be built on top or gardens and play space laid out."

This proposal, which would ruin much of Hampstead and Camden Town (and be the cause of blight and then roadworks for at least thirty years) was the best that the road lobby and County Hall councillors and traffic engineers could come up with – but it did bask in the support of transport guru Professor Colin Buchanan, to whom roads appear to have been not only a means but an end in themselves. The scheme was as damaging to the environment, which the road planners protested they were trying to preserve, as the absurd plan, mooted later, to drive major roads through Covent Garden once the fruit and veg market had relocated.

This County Hall hubris, however, meant that a lot of people had to spend a lot of time opposing it – protesters included Camden Council, local MPs and many other people, especially the Hampstead Motorway Action Group. The latter, formed in 1966, must take much of the credit for the abandonment of the scheme and the thanks of present-day Camden Town residents. Needless to say, the scheme could not have been afforded, let alone desired,

124. A public warning against knocking off caps. (See next page)

and when Labour regained the GLC in 1973 the plan was quietly aborted, though in case Labour were triumphant about that they should have been reminded that it was the Labour LCC and GLC that proposed it in the first place.

Music Places

Second only to the West End in choice of music venues, Camden Town has a remarkable reputation for its variety. It ranges from folk music at Cecil Sharp House, hard rock, goth and punk at numerous places and jazz at the Jazz Café. As Camden Lock market became better known – well before the explosion of markets we see today – Dingwall's at the Lock was the main musical attraction. Today it has many rivals including the Koko nightclub at the old **Camden Theatre** near Mornington Crescent underground station, the **Electric Ballroom** (see separate section), and the World's End (the old Mother Red Cap pub) with its basement attraction the Underworld. But there are many smaller places specialising in different types of pop music.

In contrast the comfortable Café Bartok at 78-79 Chalk Farm Road plays modern classical and crossover music, the Black Cap at 171 Camden High Street is well known for its drag entertainment, and the Dublin Castle at 94 Parkway is, of course, known for its Irish music.

A festival of many types of music, called the Camden Crawl, which began in 1995, takes place each April.

North London Collegiate School for Boys

This school predated Miss Buss's famous **North London Collegiate School for Girls** by a few months. But, established in January 1850, it lasted just fifty years, while the Girls' school, with a mission other than commercial, was to go on to be a leading school. The Boys' school was established by Frederick Waymouth at 6

91

Camden High Street.

The proprietor advertised that it "is conducted under the general superintendence of the Vicar and Clergy of St Pancras, and is divided into two departments – the Mercantile or Commercial Department, and the Classical or Professional Department, the course of study of the former having direct reference to Mercantile life, and that in the latter to Professions, entrance at the Universities, and all those stations in life for which a good general Education is required."

This status did not prevent the pupils suffering some abuse, for a public notice posted in 1857 stated that: "J. Osborn was this day COMMITTED TO PRISON by the Magistrate at Clerkenwell, for throwing Stones, and knocking off the Caps of the Pupils of the North-London Collegiate School. And all Boys causing annoyance, are hereby Cautioned that the Magistrate is determined to punish with the utmost severity of the law, the next Offender brought before him." *(See ill. 124)*

Tuition fees were £2.7s per quarter "beyond which there are no extras, except for Drawing and Printed Books".

In 1866 the *Camden and Kentish Town Gazette* reported on a prize-giving at the school:

"St Martin's Hall was filled yesterday with the parents and friends of the pupils of this excellent school, which has rose [sic] from a small beginning of some nineteen scholars to 400 … The Rev Canon Humphreys presided, and after stating the proud position the school had attained, said that no pains would be spared by himself or his colleagues to render the school efficient."

By 1868 the school had moved to 12 Camden High Street and can be seen in a photograph with pupils looking out at the unveiling of the **Cobden** statue.

Despite its patronage the school appears to have closed in the 1890s, probably short of pupils once state education had got into its stride.

The author and entertainer, George Grossmith (1847-1912), was a pupil at the school.

North London Collegiate School for Girls

Frances Mary Buss (1827-94), founder of the North Collegiate School for Girls and of **Camden School for Girls**, was born into an artistic family and spent her childhood in a house in Mornington Crescent. Her father, Robert, illustrated books and lectured on art. Her own education was at a dame school in Mornington Place, Hampstead Road, run by a Mrs Wyand, and at the age of 18 she began working in a school in Kentish Town that her mother ran. The curriculum was quite advanced for girls' schools – it included languages, art and science.

Miss Buss realized that the education available for middle class girls was woeful. Social prestige prevented them from attending church schools with the poorer children of the neighbourhood, and fathers quite often felt that it was a waste of time to educate them at all. They might have a governess, sometimes adequate and sometimes not, and that was the extent of it. Governesses, usually spinsters with few prospects in life, were becoming numerous and exploited, to the extent that the Governesses' Benevolent Institution was founded in 1843 with the aim of raising their status. (The Institution was later to build their headquarters in Prince of Wales Road, which later became the home of the Camden School for Girls.) In Miss Buss's day, middle-class girls were expected to learn enough to be a considerate and competent wife and mistress of a household. It was this attitude that Miss Buss at a young age was determined to challenge and to change.

Her aspirations were helped considerably by her knowing the Rev. David Laing, vicar of Holy Trinity in West Kentish Town, who was also the secretary of the Governesses' Institution. He encouraged Miss Buss to attend classes at the new Queen's College in Harley Street; here she was a fellow pupil of Dorothy Beale, the future Principal of Cheltenham College for Ladies.

At the age of 22 Miss Buss, confident that she had sufficient education and experience of teaching, opened the North London School for Ladies on 4 April 1850 at the family home at 46 Camden Street. The family occupied the basement and attics, and Miss Buss had her office in the parlour room. By December of that year, she had 115 pupils crowded into the house, their parents attracted by the moderate fees. Her father taught art and science, two of her brothers provided Latin and Arithmetic, and the Rev. Laing gave religious tuition. In all this Frederick Denison Maurice, founder of the **Working Men's College** helped.

It was not long before the school outgrew this modest house and moved to new premises at 207 Camden Road, by Sandall Road, leaving

125. *The gymnasium at the North London Collegiate School for Girls.*

Camden Street free for Miss Buss's new creation, Camden School for Girls. With generous donations from private individuals and City livery companies, the North London Collegiate bought a furniture store in Sandall Road and on 29 June 1880, a new building was opened by the Archbishop of York.

Once more the school outgrew its premises and with a courageous leap the school moved out of what was then London to the end of the northern line at Edgware where Canons, the former mansion of the 1st Duke of Chandos, lay empty and up for sale. By that time many of the school's pupils came from Middlesex rather than London, and the Middlesex County Council made a

donation to help the purchase in May 1929. The whole school moved to Canons in 1938 – and just in time, for the old school in Sandall Road was devastated by bombing in the 2nd World War.

The North London Collegiate remains at Canons and is today one of the most prestigious girls' schools in the country.

North London Line

The North London Line, at the moment known as Silverlink, is *in the Camden area* a combination of two lines, although its historical relationship with other short lines is much more complex than that. The first part of the line was the prosaically named East and West India Docks and Birmingham

Junction Railway. The purpose of this as indicated in its title – was to move goods brought into the London & North Western Railway's depot at Camden Town and transport them to the London Docks, in effect mirroring the route of the Regent's Canal. The line from Camden Town was fully opened in 1850 and was intended at first to be primarily a freight railway. Its name was changed to the North London Railway on 1 January 1853. The first station south on what was then popularly known as the Camden Town Railway was Camden Road, then on the opposite side of the viaduct. A long report in the *Illustrated London News* in 1851 describes a journey from Blackwall to Camden Town. Nearing our area it relates:

126. *The North London Line crossing at Camden Road station, c.1905.*

"Through the high level of Islington the railway is in a cutting averaging 16ft deep with walls of massive brickwork. We quit this cutting near the Caledonian road, and cross the same by a bridge ... We next passed over the Great Northern Railway; and it was a curious sight to see a monster Northern train, sixty feet below us, entering the tunnel running under the extensive tract of land known as Copenhagen fields. This is indeed one of the most singular views through which the railway passes.

"After passing several beautiful villas we arrived at Camden Town, where the railway is constructed on a brick viaduct of good proportions. We soon enter upon ground intersected with the rails of the Great North-Western Railway until we reach the end of our journey at the Hampstead Road [Primrose Hill]."

Camden Road station was opened on 7 December 1850. It was near here that a serious accident occurred on 16 August 1864, when a passenger train boiler exploded, forcing the engine off the viaduct behind Randolph Street, though fortunately the carriages remained on the track. Six years later the station was elegantly rebuilt by Edwin Henry Horne – he designed a number in this style along the line, such as Canon-bury, sadly demolished in recent years.

In 1860 the Hampstead Junction Railway was constructed. It began right next to the North London Railway just west of the railway bridge crossing Kentish Town Road and went generally westward to Kentish Town West, Gospel Oak and Hampstead Heath, and eventually on to Willesden and Richmond.

The North London through Camden crosses at rooftop level, and certainly had a deleterious effect around Camden Road station. However it was nowhere near as bad as the line proposed by the London Grand Junction Railway in 1838, which also had as its purpose to move goods from Camden Town to the Docks. Its line would have gone, most likely at roof top level, in a south-east direction from the Goods Yard, over Arlington Road, the High Street and a number of streets to the east of that, and then on down past the front of St Pancras Old Church.

The North London is due to be taken over by Transport for London in November 2007 and, hopefully, it will not be called Silverlink any more.

North London School of Drawing and Modelling

This school was on the north side of Mary Terrace, the alleyway connecting the High Street and Arlington Road, in which once was the entrance to the Bedford Music Hall. According to the *Illustrated London News* in 1852, it was a "Suburban Artizan School" aimed at the

127. The North London School of Drawing and Modelling. From the Illustrated London News, *17 January, 1852.*

"superior class of skilled workmen". It had Prince Albert as a patron and as president the ubiquitous Rev. David Laing.

North West London Hospital

At the rear of the Sainsbury car park entrance in Kentish Town Road was once St James's Terrace. At nos 18 and 20 (later extended to 24) was established in 1878 the North West London Hospital, with Princess Christian as patron. Its major work was with sick children, and it dealt with 600 in-patients a year. It merged with Hampstead Hospital on Haverstock Hill in 1907 and in-patients were treated there, while out-patients were still dealt with in Camden Town.

In 1912 a new out-patient building opened in Greenland Road. This building is still there and displays the two signs above doorways: 'Entrance to Out-patients' and 'Entrance to Casualties'. Treatment was free to the sick poor. Today the old hospital is used by the Greenland Road Children's Centre.

Old St Pancras Church House

No. 26 Crowndale Road is now the venue for the Greek theatre, **Theatro Technis**, but it was once the mission house and vicarage of Old St Pancras Church in Pancras Road. Above the doorway was a statue purporting to be of St Pancras, the young Roman martyr who died for his faith *c.* AD304. This was stolen in 2000 and replaced by a replica, carved by Jim Staines, in 2001.

The building was opened in 1897, replacing the Crowndale

Hall which had once served as an inadequate coroner's court. That hall was so small that, as reported in a local newspaper, the coroner and his staff conducting an inquest had to stand out in the street while the jury considered their verdict in privacy. A new coroner's court (and Mortuary) were opened in St Pancras Gardens in 1888, and most likely the Hall was used by the Royal Veterinary College until it was demolished and the mission house built.

Theatro Technis have been in the building since 1978.

Oetzmanns

In the 19th century London had two centres of furniture shops. One was Wardour Street, the other in or around Tottenham Court Road. In the latter street were Maples, the largest sup-

129. *Our Lady of Hal in Arlington Street, in the 1930s.*

128. *Oetzmann's cabinet works at the south-eastern end of Camden High Street, north of the Camden Theatre.*

plier of furniture in the country, Heal's and Shoolbred's. But at nos 62, 64 and 67-79 Hampstead Road, near the junction with Euston Road, was Oetzmann's, who sold large quantities of rather down-market, but solid furniture. They proudly advertised branches in Dublin and, oddly, Ryde, Isle of Wight. Perhaps the latter branch was intended to help furnish Osborne, Queen Victoria's mansion there. At the coronation of 1902 the firm produced a catalogue that sold bunting and flags, as well as 20,000 'solid oak chairs'. Abundant furniture, usually walnut or mahogany, suited Victorian and Edwardian taste, and it was relatively cheap – at the end of the 19th century Oetzmann's were advertising

sideboards for 8 guineas, dining tables at 55 shillings and couches from 38 shillings and sixpence. In 1945 the firm bought the old Tattersall auction premises at Knightsbridge Green and used them as a furniture gallery.

Oetzmann's, at the peak of their production in 1897, took over the old premises of the **North London Collegiate School for Boys** at 12 Camden High Street for a cabinet works. This they left in 1955 and later part of the site was used as a public library.

Our Lady of Hal

This Roman Catholic church at 165 Arlington Road began as a place of worship for Belgian refugees fleeing the violence of

the 1st World War. It was under the auspices of the Scheute Order. Oddly, for such an Irish area, it was the only Catholic church in Camden Town.

Originally there was a temporary building on the east side of the street, on the site of today's church hall, but a purpose-built church was opened in 1933, designed by Wilfred Mangan. Inside is a memorial to Albert I, King of the Belgians. Hal is a place west of Brussels in which there is a notable shrine to the Virgin Mary.

The Belgian priests were recalled to Belgium in 1982 and administration was transferred to the Catholic Diocese of Westminster.

Oval Road

Oval Road is straight. The original plan, it is usually stated, was to build two crescents their back gardens facing each other, with Oval Road bisecting the oval they formed. Gloucester Crescent was built as from 1840, but the railway had already intruded on the plan, and the western part of the 'oval' was not built. This seems a reasonable solution to the street name's derivation but this author has some reservations. The railway was constructed some years before any streets were laid out or houses built. The sale notice map of 1840 published by the Southampton Estate when it sold the area for development, at least three years after the line had been extended to Euston, has Gloucester Crescent planned and named, but not built. What is now Oval Road is shown, unbuilt, but not named. It depicts how the railway cuts across on the western side, prohibiting the building of another crescent. Why then, at that stage, name the straight road Oval?

In any event the railway effectively prevented some houses being built on the western side of Oval Road – only in land hungry modern times a number have been added right near the railway bridge.

Oval Road led into **Gilbeys'** yard and the canal area; a potato warehouse was on the west side at the northern end on a site now being redeveloped as Lockhouse. On the east side there are a few conventional houses and also **Regent's Park Terrace**, a complete development in itself and somehow oddly placed here, set back from the road.

Palmer's Pet Store

At the time of writing (June 2007) George Palmer's old pet store at 35 Parkway is empty and has been for some time since this well-known business transferred to the opposite side of the road, leaving behind a splendid fascia advertising monkeys, talking parrots and naturalists. It will be interesting to see if any newcomer in those premises has to keep, under listed building legislation, this charming reminder of a business. The new shop is

much more mundane and confined to less exotic creatures.

George Palmer, who became a Fellow of the Zoological Society, set up at 35 in 1918 and was able, in those less regulated days, to cage and sell animals that would be off limit today. Begun as a 'livestock' shop (with the telegraphic address of 'Domestipet'), in modern times it claimed to be the oldest pet store in the world. The manager appeared in a press photograph in 1969 with a boa constrictor, and the information that the snake and her 20 young snakes were set loose in the shop at night to deter burglars.

A 1933 letter from Palmer's

survives in the archives of the Royal Veterinary College, asking the College to find out what was wrong with some monkeys they had delivered there.

Park Chapel

The Congregationalists had a strong presence in Camden and Kentish Towns. Park Chapel at the corner of Arlington Road and Delancey Street (west side) was the principal Congregational church in Camden Town. Its first building opened in 1843, supported by the Metropolis Chapel Fund. The Rev. Joshua Harrison was its minister for 45 years. How-

130. Park Chapel, early 20th century.

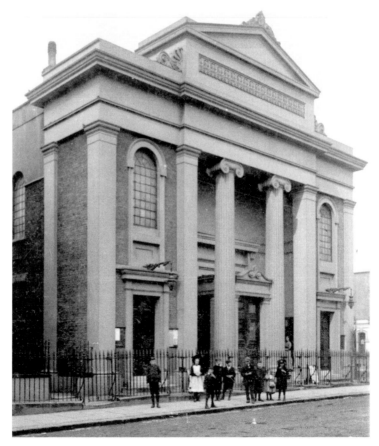

131. The fire at the Park Theatre in Parkway in 1881, from The Penny Illustrated Paper.

ever, five years after it was built, the chapel was destroyed by fire – it was rebuilt in five months, much grander, with ionic columns in the portico and with 1,500 seats. This building was destroyed by bombing in the last war and local authority housing (Ruscombe) now occupies the site.

Park Theatre

The Park Theatre was on the site of the Odeon cinema in Parkway. Originally called the Royal Alexandra Theatre, it opened on 31 May, 1873 under the management of a musician called Thorpe Pede. It cost £20,000 to build. There was a façade three storeys high in Italianate style, a double flight of steps up from the street, and then two staircases to all parts of the theatre (which included boxes), except for the gallery which was approached from the side in Arlington Road.

The usual fare was melodrama or operetta, quite often imported from the West End. Sir Herbert Beerbohm Tree made some of his earliest performances here. The theatre was taken over in 1877 by a Madame St Claire who, apart from dabbling in séances, produced *Romeo and Juliet*, with herself as Romeo and her daughter as Juliet.

Though the *Sporting & Dramatic News* in 1878 remarked that it was a "pretty suburban house", a theatre writer in 1925 was a bit more sniffy: "It was quite a pleasant little house which I remember very well, but must be considered as one of the least notable of all London theatres."

It became the Park Theatre by 1879, but on 11 September

1881 it burnt down, as so many theatres did, despite the attentions of the fire brigade. Fifty horses, stabled in Inverness Street behind, were moved for safety.

The theatre was not rebuilt, but was replaced by the Royal Park Hall that was used for functions and one-off entertainments; this was later converted into workshops. In 1937 the Gaumont cinema was built on its site. (*See* **Cinemas**)

Park Villages

The villas of Park Village East and West adorned each bank of the spur of the Regent's Canal that led down to the **Cumberland Basin**. They were designed in the 1820s and 1830s by John Nash and his pupil and relative, James Pennethorne, in a style reminiscent of the model village Nash had built at Blaise Hamlet in Gloucestershire. Sir John Summerson commented that "Building this essay in the picturesque compensated him for having to leave out the clusters of villas he planned for the park itself. Trees, water, fanciful gables and balconies – all the properties of the romantic village scene as illustrated in the almanacs and the keepsakes are here."

Park Village West, in the triangle between Albany Street, the barracks and the Regent's Canal spur, is still intact though nos. 15 and 16 had to be extensively rebuilt because of war damage. Small villas are grouped around a horseshoe shaped road. The most notable is no. 12, Tower House, in Italianate style, probably built just before 1837. Its first occupier was Dr James Johnson, physician to both William IV

and to Nash himself; from 1848-52 the house was occupied by that painter of vast scenes, W.P. Frith. Later residents have included the politician and journalist, Woodrow Wyatt, and the couturier Norman Hartnell. James Wyld, a celebrated geographer, who displayed a vast model of the earth, 60ft in diameter, in Leicester Square in 1851, was at no. 8.

This small enclave once had a louche reputation. In Michael Sadleir's novel *Fanny by Gaslight*, it is portrayed as Florizel, a place for ladies of easy virtue. This may be true, for the writer, Gillian Tindall, has found that a house in Park Village East was observed in 1905 to have had within four days visits from 41 couples, most of whom left after staying a short time.

Park Village East, a larger complex of buildings, had villas on both sides of the road, but those on the eastern side were swept away by railway expansion in 1906. No. 1, on the east side, was once a riding school – hence the statue of a horse still at the front – and more latterly a film studio in a building constructed in the garden of the **York & Albany**

132. Tower House in Park Village West.

133. Park Village East, from the Regent's Canal. In the foreground are the rear elevations of nos. 6-8. Drawing by Thomas H Shepherd., c.1829.

*134. In reverse, the fronts of the same buildings from the street, also by Shepherd, c.1829. On the right in the distance is the **York & Albany** with its colonnade which was taken down when the pub exterior was extended to cover the space it enclosed.*

pub – the latter is now being converted after years of dereliction and delay by the Crown Estate. A number of villas have been lost on the other side of the road as well, notably those damaged in the war and replaced by Nash House, an architecturally dubious tribute to the great man. That redoubtable Fabian, Sidney Webb was at no. 4 in 1889, and the left-wing journalist and writer, Charlotte Haldane, was at no. 16 in 1934.

Parkway

On the *c*.1800 map of the parish of St Pancras a track called Crooked Lane runs on the line of today's Parkway down to the boundary of Marylebone Fields – what became Regent's Park. It is an odd track, since it led to nowhere – it just stopped at that boundary. The only buildings in the lane were very near the High Street. On the north side was **Britannia** Field, named after the pub in the High Street. By 1834, after the creation of Regent's Park, the track, now a road, was inevitably known as Park Street, and then it was changed to Parkway in an overall renaming of the numerous 'Park Streets' by the London County Council.

Before and after the last war the road was a general shopping street, but in the last twenty years has become a thoroughfare of restaurants, estate agents and boutique shops, complementing the populist Camden Markets nearby and the rather down-market High Street to the south. The Dublin Castle is at no. 94 but the Windsor Castle at 32, has disappeared. The Spread Eagle on the corner with Albert Street has become the Earl of Camden, but The Camden Stores on the corner with Arlington Road, not an inspiring name, was ineptly renamed the Rat and Parrot and is at the time of writing being renovated. The Regent Bookshop at no. 73 has, sadly, departed. No. 5 was once a Barclay's Bank, and is now the well-established Jazz Café, run by the Mean Fiddler organization. Robertson's, who made up artists' colours, opened up a shop at no. 71 in 1936 and left in the 1980s. Founded in 1810, they had been previously in Long Acre, and had made up paints for the Pre-Raphaelites. **Palmer's** famous pet stores have moved across the road from their decorative old address.

The mainly glass building (at the time of writing, empty) at the corner with Gloucester Avenue, was once a Henley's car showroom. It was remodelled in 1983 as Design House and used by media firms.

There is an interesting group of buildings on the south side, around Ranelagh Mews entered from Parkway; here at one

135. *Parkway c.1904. Nos 39-40 are immediately to the left, and the view is looking east to the junction with Arlington Road.*

136. The Parkway junction with Camden High Street, c.1905. The Britannia is on the corner. We are looking south-west.

time were the celebrated music printers Lowe & Brydon. In the early days of music printing each note was painstakingly etched on to stone, whereas nowadays it is easily done on a computer. The main buildings have been remodelled by the architects Sheppard Robson & Partners, who have their practice here.

Piano making

The pianoforte (meaning soft-loud) enabled musicians to add subtlety to their performances, and the invention of the upright piano, as we know it, in 1800 brought the instrument into thousands of domestic parlours. In England, piano manufacture was concentrated in north London, especially in Camden and Kentish Towns, and along the Regent's Canal which facilitated the import of heavy timber and then, via the

canal system again, transportation of the finished instruments inland and, via the London docks, abroad. In Camden by 1884 there were fifty firms, large and very small, working in the piano industry.

Collard and Collard, described in a separate entry in this book, were the principal piano manufacturers in Camden Town, rivalling the famous Brinsmead company in Grafton Road, Kentish Town.

137. One of the many small suppliers in the locality who made parts for the major piano builders.

FOR ALL PIANOFORTE ACCESSORIES, SCREWS, WREST PLANKS, CROSSWAY, BARWOOD, &c.

SERVICE SECOND TO NONE

ONE QUALITY ONLY GOODS STOCKED THE BEST

HECKSCHER & CO.
75, Bayham Street, Camden Town, N.W.1

TELEPHONE No.: EUSTON 1735

THE ONLY MANUFACTURERS OF WREST PINS IN THE UNITED KINGDOM

ESTABLISHED 1883

Another local firm was Chappell's, founded by Samuel Chappell in 1811, as music publishers, concert agents and, later, pianoforte manufacturers. Chappell's first factory was in Chalk Farm Road, but also had premises in Ferdinand Street and Berkley Road, Chalk Farm.

In Curnock Street, Camden Town, the firm of Charles Challen, probably founded in the 1820s, had a factory. This company specialized in baby grands and at one time received from the BBC the largest order for concert grands in the history of piano manufacturing.

Pickford's

The website for Pickford's, the carriers, claims that the company originated in 1695, and certainly by 1756 James Pickford had two depots in London. He invested in fly wagons for speed on roads, carrying goods and passengers, and could cover London to Manchester in 4½ days. The company's dominance in the carrier trade began with its use of canals, a network of which gradually found its way down to Paddington and, when the Regent's Canal was constructed, via Camden Town to the London docks. At that time Camden Town was of no importance to Pickford's, because the railway had not yet been built, and so their main London wharf was at the City Road Basin, further east on the canal. Travel on canals was slow, though the use of fly boats, which had precedence over other craft, helped matters. By 1838 Pickford's had 120 boats of their own, and the journey from Birmingham to London took 2½ days. When the first trains ran, it took ten hours.

The Pickford family got into financial difficulties and in 1817 sold the business to Joseph Baxendale and his part-ners. It was he that brought the firm to the eminence it enjoyed in the 19th century.

When the London & Birmingham Railway (**London & North Western**) was built with a goods yard at Camden Town in the mid 1830s, not only did Pickford's move their main warehouse from the City Road to Camden but by 1850 had withdrawn from the use of canals altogether. The company bought a plot of land on the south side of the canal at the end of Oval Road, and William Cubitt designed for them a building in which goods could be interchanged between canal, rail and road. This opened in 1841 and was rebuilt in 1857 after a serious fire. Much of Pickford's business stemmed from their relation-ship with the railway at Camden, but in 1901 they broke with the L&NWR – there had been a dispute as to which company owned the Pickford wag-

138. *The Pickford's depot at Camden Town.*

139. Fire at Pickford's depot in 1857. We are looking north up Oval Road. Many horses were rescued and they stampeded in terror into the surrounding streets

ons attached to freight trains. In the 1880s they moved out of their large depot at Camden, leaving it to **Gilbeys'**. In 1912 Pickford's merged with their biggest rival, Carter Paterson, and in 1947 road carrying was nationalized for some years. In 1982 there was an employee buyout of the whole company which, by then, included several other firms.

During the canal and railway heyday, Pickford's relied very heavily on horses, and by 1919 had 1900 horse-drawn vehicles in London, and 1580 horses. Horses were used into the 1960s, but by the end of the 1930s most of Pickford's fleet was motorised.

The Pirate Castle

On the Regent's Canal near Camden Lock is an odd, castellated, fortress-like building designed in an uncharacteristic style by Tony Henderson, a partner in the firm of Richard Seifert, whose tower blocks in the 1960s and 1970s dominated new London buildings. It is the headquarters of a charity which began with Viscount

St Davids (a local resident), aided by Paddy Walker (*see* **Jenny Wren**), teaching young people how to use the canal safely for recreation. The venture began on 6 March 1966, and at first used a barge called *Rosedale* as its base, with a number of boats, rowing or canoe, stored in St Davids' garden which ran down to the canal from St Mark's Crescent. *Rosedale* was fitted out

with changing rooms for boys and girls, an office and a clubroom. Viscount St Davids ran this club virtually singlehanded for most of the time, but gradually trained others to take responsibility for newcomers and younger members.

Disaster came when *Rosedale* was destroyed by arson in 1968. The club somehow continued and the Pirate Castle building was opened in 1977 on land donated by Camden Council. It was used by schools during term time, and by members of the club during holidays and weekends. By 1983 the club had 35 craft. There have been funding problems in recent years and the club was closed for some time, reopening briefly in 2003. Substantial refurbishment of the Castle is underway and the organization expects to reopen once more in the summer of 2008 when, apart from activities on the canal, the building will provide a community centre for young people.

140. The Pirate Castle on the Regent's Canal.

Playing cards in Camden Town

From a factory behind Royal College Street, the firm of Charles Goodall for many years produced more playing cards than the other firms in the country combined. By 1845 Goodall's and De la Rue produced two thirds of all cards made in England.

The Goodall family moved to London by 1796, and lived in St Marylebone. Their son, Charles (1785-1851), was apprenticed to Hunt & Sons, cardmakers of 29 Piccadilly and remained there until 1820 when he set up his own business in Lisle Street, Soho. He moved to 30 Great Pulteney Street six years later, and in 1833/4 he leased 12-18 Royal College Street, some of the first houses and shops built on the east side of that street, just a

CHAS. GOODALL & SON.

PRIZE MEDALS.

LONDON, 1862.	MELBOURNE, 1880.
PARIS, 1867.	ADELAIDE, 1881.
PHILADELPHIA, 1876.	CHRISTCHURCH, 1882.
PARIS, 1878.	AMSTERDAM, 1883.
SYDNEY, 1879.	CALCUTTA, 1884.

Wholesale and Export Stationers.

MANUFACTURERS OF

PLAYING CARDS,

Mounting Boards, Ivory Boards and Cards, Ticket Boards, Cardboards, Message Cards, Bristol Boards, Carte-de-Visite & Photographic Mounts.

❈ CALENDARS ❈

Ball Programmes & Menu Cards.

MEMORIAL CARDS.

141. Below, the yard at Goodall's factory in Royal College Street. 142, above, an advertisement for some of their products.

105

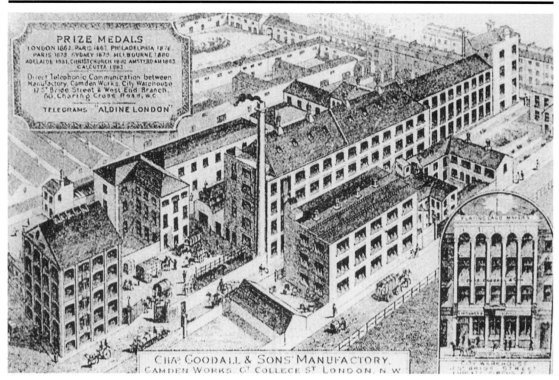

143. Goodall's factory between Royal College Street and St Pancras Way. It was entered through number 24.

little up from the Royal Veterinary College. Goodall's soon expanded and the firm later took in nos. 20 and 22 plus a former gun factory on land behind, which ran down to the Fleet river.

The firm's productivity increased enormously in the 1850s when stamp duty on a pack of cards was reduced from one shilling to threepence.

Goodall's also produced calendars, writing paper and envelopes. Less likely, the firm marketed a lavatory paper holder. Their publicity boasted: "By an ingenious method of packing this paper, it is impossible that more than one sheet can be detached at a time, and thus this most serious source of waste is avoided."

More land was acquired there and a new factory built behind nos 20-32, with the main entrance at 24. The company was so large that it had twenty horse-drawn delivery vans, and by 1913 Goodall's were producing 2 million packs per annum – all other British manufacturers produced only 648,000 packs between them.

For several reasons, the firm declined in the twentieth century and in 1921 it was sold to old rivals De la Rue and though the Goodall name was kept on this too lapsed in the 1970s. The site of their factory is now covered by the large Royal Mail depot.

The Goodall family home in the more prosperous times was Linden House at 1 The Grove, Highgate Road, opposite Grove Terrace.

Poets in Camden Town

The Yeats family, headed by the artist father John, spent some years off and on at 23 Fitzroy Road, Chalk Farm between 1868 and 1874, before they moved to West Kensington. The future poet, William Butler Yeats (1865-1939) was only about three when he came to no. 23, and his brother, Jack Yeats (1871-1957), who became a noted artist, was born there. A plaque relating to William Butler is on the house, just as there is on 5 Woburn Walk near Euston Station, where he lived from 1895 to 1919.

No. 23 was also the address of the American poet Sylvia Plath (1932-63), who moved here with her two children in December 1962 after the break up of her marriage with the

106

144. *Dylan Thomas and his landlady by the caravan he used in Delancey Street.*

poet Ted Hughes. The two of them had previously lived in the fourth floor flat of 7 **Chalcot Square** from January 1960.

Though she was riding high in professional terms, Plath was extremely depressed by her marriage breakdown, and this could not have been helped by the severe winter of 1962/3. She took her own life at no. 23 on 12 February 1963.

A blue plaque also adorns 54 Delancey Street, where the Welsh poet Dylan Thomas (1914-53) stayed from November 1951 until January 1952. He professed not to have liked it there and described it as "Our new London house of horror on bus and night lorry route and opposite railway bridge and shunting station". He was a frequent visitor to the Camden

145. *William Butler Yeats. Charcoal drawing by J S Sargent.*

Street library and did not return the last three books he borrowed. In the back garden in Delancey Street he worked in a caravan – this has recently been renovated.

Presbyterians

The Trinity Reformed Church in Buck Street is on the site of the Congregational Ebenezer Chapel, founded by a High Street upholsterer, Thomas William Gittens, in 1835. (A Gittens Brothers, upholsterers, was still at 112-114 High Street in 1922). Gittens was very much a fundamentalist in his approach, kindly summed up in Miller's history of St Pancras (1874): "The style of Mr Gittens' preaching, though not claiming to be of much cultivation, was impressive and calculated to reach the heart ... While discoursing on the love of God as exhibited to a sinful world by the gift of His beloved Son, he has occasionally been overcome by his emotions, and tears

146. An advertising postcard for the Presbyterian church in Camden Park Road.

have rolled down his face, and the congregation could not fail to be deeply impressed by his theme ... his language was fluent, and he greatly improved his natural gifts during his ministry."

The chapel closed in 1874 and it was sold to the Presbyterians, who renamed it Trinity Church. This had to be rebuilt after a fire just before the 1st World War. Nationally, the Presbyterian Church and the Congregational Church merged in 1972 to become the United Reformed Church.

The largest Presbyterian church in Camden Town was that in Camden Park Road – the building is still there, but with a stunted tower that is now incongruously festooned with aerials. The foundation stone of this church, designed by Finch, Hill & Paraire, was laid in 1869, with the Rev. William Dinwinnie as its first minister. It was damaged during the last war, abandoned as a place of worship, and used as a scenery painting warehouse. Latterly it has been refurbished as Church Studios and is used by hi-tech companies.

Primrose Hill

Most of the wasteland that was once Primrose Hill was owned by Eton College from 1449 when it acquired, as a gift from Henry VI, the Chalcots estate in Hampstead. The rest, on the eastern – Chalk Farm – fringes was part of the estate of Lord Southampton. The name, Primrose Hill, has been used since the 15th century.

As development crept up from London, lapping at the foot of the hill, so the temptation to both landowners to develop the hill was strong. In the event, when Eton College proposed c. 1840 to cover the hilltop, popular agitation prevented it and instead its ground was taken over by the Crown in exchange for some land at Windsor. In 1842 an Act of Parliament preserved what was left of the hill – Southampton had already built on some of it – and created a park for the public. The hill, 206ft above sea level, needed a great deal of improvement. A writer on its history notes that before management by the Crown Estate "Owing to the want of adequate drainage, the hillsides were cut into deep and dangerous ravines, while the lower grounds, especially on the western side, were hardly passable by reason of the ponds and pools of water which accumulated in the hollow grounds. All this has now disappeared, deep and dangerous holes have been levelled over, and bare patches of the hillside covered with grass."

Miller, in his 1874 history of St Pancras, notes that "Forty, thirty, even but twenty years ago, Primrose Hill was the resort of the roughest and rudest classes of people, at holiday time and on Sundays. A certain class of caterers for the bodily wants of the multitude then made a din with their cries, the remembrance of which contrasts most unfavourably with the conduct of the orderly law-abiding people who now frequent the hill and repose on the grass or on the excellent seats around its summit."

The writer also refers to the reputation the hill had for

147. *Primrose Hill in the 1890s.*

duelling. The most notable contest was that between a man called Scott, who was editor of the *London Magazine*, and another named Christie. In this Scott was killed. This did not help the reputation of the area, for the memory of the famous discovery of the body of Sir Edmond Bury Godfrey in 1678 still lingered (*see* **Chalk Farm Tavern**).

Even before development was proposed, the hill was saved from a rather bizarre scheme. In 1829, a Thomas Willson announced a project to burrow into the hill to form a cemetery which would take five million bodies – this at a time when the shortage of space in parish burial grounds had reached scandalous levels. Willson proposed that the cemetery would be in the shape of a pyramid, resting on a square about the size of Russell Square, and with a height beyond that of St Paul's. He proclaimed that his "grand Mausoleum will go far towards the glory of London" and that "every deposit" would be "hermetically sealed for ever".

Ragged Schools

From the *Illustrated London News*, 5 August 1848:

"On Monday evening a public meeting was held at the new vestry-rooms, St Pancras-road, on behalf of the Camden-town Ragged Schools; Lord Ashley, M.P., in the chair. The report set forth the necessity of establishing ragged schools in Camden-town, and stated that a spot was selected in Little Camden-street, and two schools were opened about three week since, capable of holding two hundred children. The sum collected was £115. 3s.; the alteration and repairs of the school amounted to £100, and a further outlay of £30 was required. The annual salaries and incidental expenses would amount to £60; and if an infant school were established, the expenses would be increased to £100 annually. The schools have been opened three weeks, and seventy children have been admitted. The children will receive a sound Scriptural education, and two industrial classes are formed twice a week. The girls are taught the art of sewing, and the boys are instructed to make and repair their own clothes."

Little Camden Street was later renamed Selous Street,

which in turn was retitled Mandela Street (*see* **Anti-Apartheid Movement**).

Rats

Celebrated in 19th-century Camden Town was Jack Black, rat and mole destroyer, and his dog Billy. He recalled:

"I should think I've been ratting a'most for five and thirty year, indeed I may say from my childhood, for I've kept at it a'most all my life... The first rats I caught was when I was about nine years of age. I ketched them at Mr Stricklands, a large cowkeeper, in Little Albany Street. At that time it was all fields and meaders in them parts ... I began with a cart and a'most a donkey, for it was a pony scarce bigger, but I've had three or four big horses since that. I used to wear a costume of white leather breeches, and a green coat and scarlet waistkit and a gold band round my hat, and a belt across my shoulder. I once went to Mr Hollins', a cowkeeper he was, where he was so infested that the cows could not lay down ... Mr Hollins gives me a recommendation to Mrs. Brown's of Camden Town, and there I sterminated above 700 rats. I was a'near being killed, for I was stooping down under the manger, when a cow heard the rats squeak, and she butts at me and sends me up again the bull. The bull was very savage, and I fainted, but I was picked up and washed, and then I came to."

Not everyone wanted their rats culled. There was a small hall in Royal College Street, which for years was the headquarters of the Southern Counties Mouse and Rat Club, established in 1915, and "affiliated in 1929 to the National Mouse and Rat Club", which held its monthly meetings there. Annual shows took place at a mission hall in Wrotham Road, off Agar Grove.

The Regent's Canal

The Grand Junction Canal, the culmination of a number of canal systems, opened its southern terminus in 1801 at Paddington, then just a village. It was the long-awaited waterway to carry goods to and from the Midlands and the North to London. Paddington, where the company constructed a large basin for wharves and agents, was as close to the metropolis as the project could manage at the time but it did have the advantage of being on the New Road, today's Marylebone-Euston-Pentonville Roads, a major highway to the City. Generally, goods destined for London Docks were offloaded on to other craft on the Thames at Brentford.

It was possible for the faster canal boats to travel from Birmingham to Paddington in 2½ days, much quicker than by road, and with bigger loads. Paddington became a large and busy distribution centre. As Jack Whitehead neatly sums it up, "As Camden Town still slept in her fields, Paddington was becoming an industrial centre."

But all this was to change. In 1802 a canal extension was proposed to link Paddington to the London Docks. In this the Grand Junction Company was involved at first but soon dropped out as they had problems of their own.

The project for this extension was carried forward by Thomas Homer and Christopher Baynes, both of whom operated boats on the Grand Junction. At the time Marylebone Park, as Regent's Park then was, though owned by the Crown was on a lease held by the Duke of Portland – but this was to expire in 1811. Before that time the Crown's agents considered just how to develop this large piece of open land so near to the West End, and these deliberations coincided with the aspirations of the Prince Regent and the availability, talent and vision of the architect, John Nash. To run the

148. Macclesfield Bridge on the Regent's Canal in the 1840s. A barge carrying gunpowder exploded early in the morning of 2 October 1874. The bridge was destroyed and three crew members lost their lives.

canal through the park became an advantage to all parties – the canal projectors got their route, albeit a longer one than they wished around the perimeter, and Nash got an ornamental feature for his new creation, the Regent's Park.

The line of the canal was on a level gradient from Paddington to Camden Town, and then via locks it went on to Islington. By the beginning of 1815 excavation was complete from Paddington to Camden Town, just before the first of several major problems struck the project. One was embezzlement by Thomas Homer, who had been appointed superintendent of the scheme. Homer skipped the country briefly and it was discovered that he had, in any case, already been declared bankrupt; worse, it was also found that his sureties were insolvent. Homer was eventually arraigned and served seven years' transportation. Two other major problems were local ones. Right from the beginning it was realized that there would be a shortage of water to supply the canal. Each time a lock is used, water is lost to the stream lower down and has to be replenished. The proprietors were therefore interested in an invention by Sir William Congreve of a lock which saved much of the water that would have been lost. It was decided to install this at Camden Town on a trial basis. However, it was a failure and meant extra cost and extra time, and in the end the Company installed conventional locks.

Then came the problem of Mr **Agar**. An irascible lawyer, he fought against the route of the canal across his land and so close to his house, Elm Lodge, roughly on the site of today's Barker Drive (named after Tom Barker, former councillor and mayor of St Pancras). In 1813 Agar discovered four or five men walking over his land surveying a route for the canal; he drove them off with some violence and then resorted to law. He had his servants put up barriers to exclude the navvies in 1815, all the while driving up the compensation price. Matters were not finally resolved until 1832, although the canal itself had opened officially and fully on 1 August 1820.

Canals everywhere diminished in importance and prosperity with the growth of the railway network. The main effect in Camden Town was that Camden Lock became prominent, situated as it was by Camden railway goods yard and there could be a mutual interchange of goods there, so convenient that **Pickford's** moved their depot from the City Road basin to Camden Town.

The canal was a nuisance when it came to the construction of the railways. Each of the Great Northern into King's Cross, the Midland into St Pancras and the London & Birmingham into Euston, had in some way to cross the canal. The best resolution of this problem was that of the Midland which went over the canal – this explains why St Pancras station is raised above ground level, with the added bonus of vast storage areas beneath the train shed into which goods could be lowered on hydraulic lifts.

Use of the Canal declined substantially after the last war as rail and road transport took away trade. Ornamental though it might have been within the perimeter of Regent's Park, it became a polluted backwater elsewhere, its waters hardly disturbed by traffic. Enthusiasts, many of them living in Camden Town, campaigned successfully for the leisure use of the canal and for its towpath to be made a public footpath.

Regent's Park Road

The road is now home to the most fashionable shops and bars in the Camden Town area, but this is fairly recent as a reader of Caroline Cooper's excellent book on local shops (*see bibliography*) will find. At the far north of them, at the junction with King Henry's Road, was the **Boys' Home**, mentioned separately in this book. South of the shops the grand houses of the road begin, mostly built in the 1840s. At no. 122 lived revolutionary Friedrich Engels (1820-95) from 1870 to 1894 where he no doubt ruminated on the distressing contrast between how the rich and the poor lived. He was visited here by the penurious Karl Marx, who lived in West Kentish Town. Engels lived here with his common-law wife Mary and, when she died in 1863, her sister moved in with him. Engels actually died at No. 41, the home of pathologist Ludwig Friedburger, but even the latest edition of the *Dictionary of National Biography* mistakenly has Engels living at that address. No 118 was the home of the Marquess de Rothwell, from whom the adjacent Rothwell Street is named.

Elegant and capacious houses faced Primrose Hill. Unfortunately many of these were swept away to build the Oldfield Estate of care apartments, named after an 1840 land owner.

At no. 90 lived 'Henry Handel Richardson' the pen name of Ethel Florence

149. The Queen's Hotel in Regent's Park Road, at the corner with St George's Terrace. The statue on the side of the pub was of Shakespeare, no doubt to complement the 'Shakespeare Oak' planted on Primrose Hill and replaced in 1964 to celebrate his 400th birthday. The pub was modernised in 1996 with an 'African' zoo theme.

Robertson (1870-1946), an Australian novelist. She was the daughter of an obstetrician and Spiritualist father whose later illness, insanity and syphilis dominated her life and he is almost certainly the subject of her best-known work, *The Fortunes of Richard Mahony*, which has established her within the Australian literary canon.

Other residents of the road have included novelists Kingsley Amis and Nigel Balchin (1908-70), who was at no. 48 from 1960 until his death.

Regent's Park Terrace

This handsome terrace of the 1840s, has had many notable occupiers. No. 12 is of particular interest. Samuel Cousins (1801-87) eminent mezzotint engraver, who became a Royal Academician, was here in the 1850s; **Louis Kossuth**, the Hungarian revolutionary, stayed here in 1861; and more recently, the critic and man of letters, V S Pritchett (1900-97) was here for 35 years. In his book *A Cab at the Door*, he recalled that his parents met at the C & A Daniels department store in Kentish Town Road, where his father was a shopwalker and his mother a milliner. In the early 1990s the house was home to David and Elizabeth Emanuel, couturiers and designers of Princess Diana's famous wedding dress. The poet Louis MacNeice (1907-63) lived at no. 10, as did the philosopher and proponent of logical positivism, A. J. (Freddie) Ayer (1910-89), in the early 1970s. The designer and restaurateur, Terence Conran (b. 1931) was here before fame and fortune in 1952, and his son, designer Jasper Conran, lived at 16 in the early 1990s. Dame Judi Dench was at no. 1 by 1967, the eminent Communist journalist, Allan Hutt (1901-1973) was at no. 8 by 1972, and Richard Whiteing (1840-1928) at no. 13 in 1910. David Thomson (1914-88) author of *The Seal* and *People of the Sea*, was at no. 22. He also wrote an autobiography called *In Camden Town*. The statistician, Claus Moser (b.1922) was at no. 3 and later took the fulsome title Baron Moser of Regent's Park in the London Borough of Camden.

The Roundhouse

The Roundhouse remarkably survives in Chalk Farm Road. It is 160 feet in diameter and its roof is supported by 24 cylindrical columns positioned towards the centre of the build-

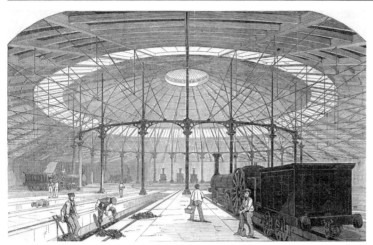

150. *The interior of the Roundhouse at the time it was an engine house in 1847.*

ing. The structure is much admired by architects and industrial archaeologists for its economic use of materials and space and is now, after the recent renovation, a magnificent auditorium for spectacle even if the spoken word can be sometimes difficult to hear.

It was built in 1847 for maintenance of the early trains of the London & North Western Railway. It could accommodate 23 engines, in bays between the columns, with one additional lane left clear for engines coming in or going out. There was a pit beneath each bay for access to the underside of the engines, and the removal of any ash. Central to the design was a 36ft turntable in the centre of the building on to which an engine would run, either to go into a berth as the turntable was rotated, or else to go into the exit lane. It was a neat solution, but the building soon became unsuitable – the received wisdom is that the turntable was too small to take the larger engines that gradually replaced the earlier models.

The late Michael Robbins, the transport historian, first at-tributed the building's design to Robert Dockray, chief assistant to Robert Stephenson and resident engineer to the London & North Western Railway – Dockray lived near the site. However, John Rapley, in a letter to the Camden History Society *Newsletter* (202), suggests that though Dockray was probably its engineer, the architect was possibly Francis Thompson, who had designed the first circular railway engine house in Derby in 1840.

After redundancy as an engine shed, the Roundhouse became a distribution centre for corn and potatoes and then a bonded warehouse for **Gilbeys'**. Gilbeys' gave up the building in 1963 when the firm moved out to Harlow.

The Roundhouse then became the home of **Centre 42** – this is dealt with in a separate section. When that organization left altogether in 1983 the freehold was bought jointly by Camden Council and the Greater London Council. A Black Arts' Centre was funded, but this venture ended acrimoniously in 1990 without much emerging from it, except re-criminations from both sides. By then a listed building, various proposals for The Roundhouse's continued use were floated, such as that of the Royal Institute of British Architects for it to house their special collections. In 1996 the building was bought by the Norman Trust, headed by Camden Town resident Torquil Norman, so that it might be transformed into a performing arts venue, mainly for young people. The Roundhouse was then used once more for theatrical performances, mainly of a musical nature, such as a revival of *Oh, what a lovely war!* and *Stomp*, and in 1999-2000 the Argentinian company, De La Guarda, had a long run here.

In 2000 the Roundhouse Trust, now the management of the building, applied for lottery funding for a fundamental renovation of the building. There were sell-out shows in 2001, and in 2002 the Royal Shakespeare Company performed *A Winter's Tale*, *The Tempest* and *Pericles*. Michael Moore presented *Michael Moore Live!*.

Reconstruction began in 2004 and the arena is now fully functional. A success in 2007 has been Tim Supple's multi-language presentation of *Midsummer Night's Dream*.

Royal College Street

The street in embryo form is shown on Thompson's *c.*1800 map of St Pancras. From south to north it crosses brickfields, which were no doubt excavated to build the houses in the vicinity. The street has some width at its southern end where the **(Royal) Veterinary College** had its new premises (*ill. 156*) together with a paddock oppo-

113

151. *The junction of the northern part of Royal College Street (left) and Kentish Town Road, in 1772, by Samuel Hieronymus Grimm. Directions to Gray's Inn and St Giles are painted on the house at the road fork. Once Camden Town was developed this spot was regarded as being the southern entry to Kentish Town.*

site on the western side. It then became a narrow track all the way to Kentish Town, with just nine houses shown just north of Plender Street. Halfway north it crosses the river Fleet.

The street, of course, takes its name from the Veterinary College, but was called *Great* College Street until 1939 when at last it caught up with the fact that the College had received its Royal charter in 1875, and the name was changed.

It was never a fashionable street and was indeed the outer limit of Lord Camden's first sporadic attempt to develop his landholdings in the area as from 1791. Some of the street on its eastern side, where the Fleet flowed between the back gardens and St Pancras Way until covered over, became light

152. *Royal College Street, c.1904. The Prince Albert pub is in the centre.*

153. *A delivery car owned by the British Tailoring and Repair Co. of Royal College Street, c.1910.*

154. *Three almost derelict houses north of the Veterinary College. In number 8, the French poets, Arthur Rimbaud and Paul Verlaine lived briefly in 1873.*

industry. At 24 was the entrance to Charles Goodall, the largest manufacturers of **playing cards** in the world in the 19th century; **Idris**, the mineral water manufacturers, had premises at 64. The College Toilet Club at 112 in the 1892 street directory, should best remain a mystery.

The street was slummy and cheap enough in the 1870s to offer accommodation for the impoverished French poets, Arthur Rimbaud and Paul Verlaine. Verlaine had left his wife and child in France and become the lover of Rimbaud as they travelled extensively in their own country and then came to England for a second time in 1873. A plaque was erected in the 1950s at no. 8, where they stayed in May and June that year, and funds are being raised to try to acquire the house from its owners, the **Royal Veterinary College**. The property, together with its two neighbours, is very derelict indeed.

Simon Callow related in *The Times* in February 2006 that the stormy relationship between Rimbaud and Verlaine eventually broke down at this address when Rimbaud made fun of Verlaine, walking along the street, carrying, of all things, kippers at arm's length. Verlaine, unamused, left the house for St Katharine Dock where he boarded a boat for Calais, followed by Rimbaud who arrived there just as the gang plank had been raised. Shortly afterwards they met in Brussels but after a long day of argument Verlaine shot Rimbaud in the wrist and was imprisoned.

The renovation and reopening of the attractive, green-tiled Prince Albert as a gastro-pub in June 2007 underlines that in some parts of Royal College Street there is a renaissance, though an unsightly generating station on the western side does not help. Oddly, the northern part of the road nearer to Kentish Town, is very down-at-heel still.

Royal Veterinary College

The College arrived in the same year –1791 – that Camden Town was first named and its development on the eastern side of the High Street began. For a nation that depended so heavily on horse power, it was odd that no such institution had been founded before – there was one in Lyons, in France, by 1762.

The College's origins lay in the Agricultural Society based in the town of Odiham in Hampshire. Its enlightened committee were concerned that the treatment of animals should be based on scientific knowledge, rather than on experience obtained from trial and error. Few of the farriers advanced enough to be known as horse-doctors were familiar with the anatomy of the horse, let alone other farm animals.

The Society's enthusiasm resulted in 1788 in the establishment of a committee which called itself the Veterinary College of London. This was chaired initially by Granville Penn, grandson of William Penn. A graduate of the Lyons establishment, Charles Vial de St Bel, offered his skills and the College advertised for a suitable piece of land. M. St Bel advised the committee not to choose marshy or low ground, because of the putrid vapours exhaled, and a site that was, from the point of view of keeping students attentive, away from the attractions of the metropolis. Lord Camden offered a site at the southern end of what became Royal College Street, with a house already on the site, and with the river Fleet flowing through the back garden. It is odd that the agents that handled the transaction asserted that the land was on an emi-

155. *The buildings of the Royal Veterinary College in Royal College Street, designed by James Burton, c.1904.*

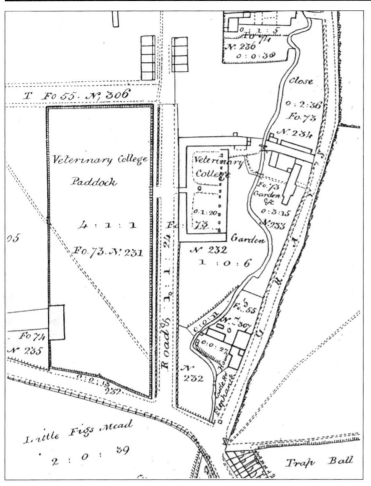

156. Thompson's map of c.1800 shows the early College premises backing on to the River Fleet. It also has a paddock across the road.

and was responsible for its development into an authoritative educational body.

Burton's original building, with its arched frontage survived into the 1930s. A student, who was at the College in 1828 described it:

"The Institution was built in a Quadrangle Form, having now in the centre a large lawn or grass plot surrounded by posts and chains, and that between the Buildings and these a broad Pathway had been left, partly paved with stones ... used chiefly for testing the freedom from lameness of Horses. In the central part of the Lawn a Mound, planted with trees and shrubs, concealed from view a large Water-tank, protected by a strong iron grating. From this source the water – needed by the whole institution – is drawn, the supply to the tank being furnished by the New River Company."

The nearest temptation to students, of the sort that worried M. St Bel, was in fact quite adjacent – the Elephant and Castle pub on the site of today's **Goldington Court**. The same student recalled that the proprietor, Mr Wrench, "will never allow more than a proper quantity of either ale, wine or spirits" to be drunk.

The location of the College was to be a fortuitous one, for it was near to both the King's Cross and Camden goods yards where hundreds of horses met with injuries during their labours.

Various buildings were added to the College over the years, but in November 1937 the present buildings, designed by Major H P Maule, were opened by George VI. These replaced the old structure and its appendages.

nence, a feature certainly not visible today and, despite M. St Bel's advice about marshy ground, it was very near indeed to Pancras Wash, just to the south, which flooded quite frequently when heavy rains added to the Fleet.

The architect James Burton was engaged to erect the first buildings, while St Bel taught the first few pupils in the house already there, which he had taken for his residence. A graduate of Lyons he may have been, but he was found to be wanting in his skills and indeed in 1789 had become well-known for his seemingly botched post-mortem on the famous racehorse of the time, *Eclipse*. (This horse was unbeaten in 18 races and when put to stud sired about 350 foals. The present Royal Veterinary College has determined that 80% of all British racehorses are descended from him.)

The irascible St Bel died at the College in 1793, in the first year that a horse was admitted for treatment.

The next principal was the autocratic Edward Coleman, who stayed in office 46 years

157. *Sainsbury's store in Camden Road, 2007.*

Sainsbury store

The Sainsbury superstore in Camden Road opened in 1988, on the site of the **ABC Bakery** and some **Artists' Studios**.

Many love its architecture, others dislike its formidable presence in the street and its domination of St Michael's church adjoining. It was designed by Nicholas Grimshaw (the architect of the Waterloo Channel Tunnel Link station). It has an enormous hall free of pillars but, as *Streets of Camden Town* points out, the frontage on Camden Road does look rather like the back of a football stadium. Even worse, it is usually filthy from traffic fumes and therefore hardly a visual asset.

Sainsbury's was founded in Drury Lane, but John Sainsbury's second shop was in Queen's Crescent, Kentish Town with a place for bacon curing nearby.

St Mark's church

This church in St Mark's Square (a square with only two sides) began as a temporary building on the site of the present 36 Regent's Park Road and 4 St Mark's Square. The foundation stone of a new church was laid in 1851, and parts of it were consecrated two years later. Most of the architecture was by Thomas Little, a contributor to its cost, but the chancel by Arthur Blomfield was finished thirty-eight years later.

St Mark's was built as part of a campaign by the energetic vicar of St Pancras, Thomas Dale, to increase the number of Anglican churches in his over-populated parish – by the

158. *St Mark's church from a bridge over the Regent's Canal, c.1904.*

118

1870s there were as many people living in St Pancras as there are today in the combined Camden borough of Holborn, Hampstead and St Pancras.

The first vicar at St Mark's was William Galloway, who completed 40 years there. Renowned for its High Church practices, Charles Booth's *Survey*, published in 1902, noted that unlike many churches which were half full, St Mark's by virtue of its 'extreme High Church practices' drew large congregations. The church also ran a National School at 179 Arlington Road. This closed in 1901 and its old building more recently has been occupied by the Cavendish School, an independent Roman Catholic school.

On 21 September 1940 the church was set alight by incendiary bombs and five nights later a high explosive bomb exploded in the chancel. The congregation then moved to Turner House in Chalcot Square, a home for blind women run by the Church Army. After July 1941 services were held in the ruined porch of the church and later in the enlarged Choir Vestry, which had escaped the fire. In 1943 a hut was opened in the church grounds and was used for services. The ruined church was extensively rebuilt after the war and consecrated on 5 October 1957. The service was attended by Sir Ninian Comper, then aged 93, whose stained glass was featured in the church.

The church was set alight again on 12 November 1994, this time by an arsonist, but the fire brigade saved the building.

There is a tradition at the church, inaugurated before the last war and enthusiastically supported by the comedians Elsie and Doris Waters ('Gert and Daisy'), who were parishioners, of selling home-made teas in the garden in the summer months.

St Mark's Crescent

This much sought-after crescent was built in the 1840s and 1850s. The gardens of one side lead down to the Regent's Canal where trade union leader Clive Jenkins once moored his boat called *The Affluent Society*, though in those days the polluted state of the canal would have made 'effluent' just as topical. Jenkins (1926-99), who lived at no. 16, was for a few years in the 1960s a St Pancras councillor who described as his recreation in *Who's Who* "organising the middle classes". On his death John Monks, General Secretary of the TUC, said that Jenkins was a one-off, "an intellectual gadly who drove forward the growth of trade unionism amongst white collar and professional workers."

At the same time, left-wing historian A J P Taylor (1906-90) lived sometimes nearby with his first wife Margaret, although he was by then married to his second wife Eve Crosland. His divorce from Margaret had been hastened by her affair with, amongst others, Dylan Thomas. Taylor had a stormy academic career, but was a notable and much admired television performer, able to deliver a long and detailed lecture without notes.

Other residents in the Crescent have included artist William Roberts (1895-1980), who was first of all a poster designer, but is remembered mostly for being a war artist in both world wars. At the Slade, where he was a student, his contemporaries included David Bomberg, Mark Gertler, Dora Carrington and Stanley Spencer. Viscount St Davids, founder of the local **Pirate Castle** youth club, lived at no. 15, on the canal side.

St Martin's Burial Ground and Almshouses

Many inner London church burial grounds were full and notoriously unhealthy by the end of the 18th century. Some Anglican churches obtained land in 'outer' London, in which the parish of St Pancras was at the time, and four burial grounds were established there, One of these was Camden Town Cemetery, used by the parish of St Martin-in-the-

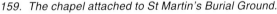

159. The chapel attached to St Martin's Burial Ground.

160. *St Martin's Burial Ground soon after its formation in 1805.*

Fields. This was opened in 1805, soon after the early development of the east side of the High Street by Lord Camden, and the almshouses, fronting Bayham Street, were added in 1817. As with each of the other three burial grounds estab- lished by outside parishes, the land acquired was designated 'extra-parochial', in other words controlled by the outside parish and beyond the jurisdiction of the host parish. This was to cause a problem in 1855 when St Martin's wished to develop for housing a portion of the ground which locals claimed had already been used for burials – St Martin's had be- fore that built on part of the unused ground in Pratt Street and Camden Street. Riots occurred and the builders were

161. *St Martin's Gardens c.1904, when the burial ground had been transformed into a public open space. The fountain on the right is now derelict.*

at the funeral of Queen Catherine in 1821, when the mob became threatening, and Dr George Swiney (*c.*1786-1844). Swiney, who lived in Arlington Road, became extremely eccentric in his later years. He did not shave for the last two of them, and his beard reached to his waist. He left instructions for his own funeral in which the main participants were to wear yellow. It has long been suggested that when St Martin's Lane by Charing Cross was widened in 1828, the bones of Nell Gwyn and the notorious highwayman and gaol-escaper, Jack Sheppard, were taken from the obliterated churchyard and re-interred in Camden Town. No evidence for this has come to light.

The Almshouses were designed by H H Steward to accommodate 70 widows and unmarried women of the parish of St Martin's. This was overcrowding but it was still forty years later before the intake was reduced to 40 after substantial adaptation of the building. A chapel was added in 1880.

St Michael's church

This church in Camden Road is a distinguished building, albeit now diminished by an unsympathetic Sainsbury's next door. The church as planned had a tower to the west, but this had to be foregone for lack of

stoned by protestors. The St Pancras medical officer of health stated that he had seen piles of bones excavated. Despite being given time to come to an amicable solution, St Martin's gave notice of recommencing the work in 1858. The matter was not resolved until 1860 when St Martin's were instructed to re-inter the remains and cease excavation.

In common with many London burial grounds, St Martin's was eventually closed and transformed into a public open space. This was opened by the Countess of Rosebery on 24 July, 1889, and at the same time she unveiled a monument to the composer, **Charles Dibdin**, who had been buried there. A helpful biographical panel about Dibdin is nearby. A fountain (now derelict) in the northeast corner was donated by the furniture firm, Maple's.

Other notables buried there have included Sir Richard Birnie, a churchwarden of St Martin's, who read the Riot Act

162. *The interior of St Michael's church, Camden Road.*

163. *Camden Road c.1905, with St Michael's church on the right. Note the rough state of the main road in those days and, to the left, the large sign advertising postcards, a popular means of communication in those days when there were several deliveries of post each day.*

164. *The St Michael's church cricket club in 1907.*

church without cover to demonstrate not only the plight of homeless people, but also hoping to persuade the public to make donations towards a full renovation of the building. Father Hunter intends that the community work of this church is "to give people living on the edge in Camden Town a new start so that, instead of being continually slapped down and moved on, they can discover their dignity and fulfil their dreams."

funds. The architect was the innovative Thomas Garner of Bodley & Garner. With the aid of funds from the sale of the site on which St Michael's Queenhithe in the City of London (hence the dedication in Camden Town), the first vicar of this newly created parish bought two houses in Camden Road and administered a temporary church here until funds were raised to erect a permanent building. The nave was completed and consecrated in 1881 and the whole church thirteen years later.

There has been recent restoration work but the church achieved national headlines in July 2006 when the current vicar, Fr. Malcolm Hunter, spent several days and nights sleeping on the roof of the

St Thomas, Wrotham Road

This is a forgotten church in a road that is now just part of a small dog leg between Agar Grove and St Pancras Way. The church is forgotten because it was demolished in the 1950s, but its history is of interest.

165. *Teulon's St Thomas's church in Wrotham Road, c.1905.*

Pancras Station. So, the church project was abandoned, but as part of Parliamentary permission to the Midland to build its line the company had to pay compensation for what had already been built in Agar Town, sufficient for the Ecclesiastical Commissioners to afford a new church a bit further north in Wrotham Road. This became St Thomas's and was consecrated in June 1863. Again, the architect was Teulon, and it was an interesting example of his style. By 1952, when the church was noticed by the *Survey of London* authors, it was derelict.

After the last war Wrotham Road was substantially truncated and the site of St Thomas's is beneath the council estate on the south side of Agar Grove.

Salvation Army

The Salvation Army building at the foot of Haverstock Hill, near Chalk Farm station, is the third in Chalk Farm. The first was behind the former petrol station just to the south in Chalk Farm Road, but the second was on the present site, opened in 1924 as part of a project to build 100 new citadels. The new building, designed by Mark Worthington, opened in 2005.

Their brass band is one of the best known of Salvation Army bands. It was formed in 1882 by Bandmaster Worbouys; in 1894 Bandmaster A W Punchard took over, and stayed in some relationship with it for 50 years. Michael Clack, who was appointed Bandmaster in 1963 was here 30 years. The band has toured the world and has played such diverse countries as Japan and the Baltic states, and played before the Pope and at Buckingham Palace.

Its origins lay in the slum district of **Agar Town** when a temporary school-cum-church was opened in 1848 for the formidable task of bringing education and religion to what was renowned, perhaps not entirely justly, as one of the poorest, dirtiest and most brutalised areas in London. It was quite near Old St Pancras church which itself was remodelled and refurbished about the same time. The new building was paid for by the Agar family which has always been much maligned for its role in the creation of Agar Town. The temporary building was superseded by another one in 1857 but the foundation stone of a permanent building was laid in 1859 at a ceremony attended by the bishop of London.

However, the new building, designed by the eminent architect Samuel Sanders Teulon, was opposed by the Midland Railway – it had many plans for the area, not the least being a line across the neighbourhood to what would be St

166. *The new Salvation Army headquarters in Haverstock Hill, with the famous band playing in the forecourt, 2007.*

Sayers, Tom

Tom Sayers (1826-1865), the celebrated pugilist, died at the home of a friend at 257 Camden High Street. He was born in a slum district of Pimlico, Brighton, and after a scanty education was apprenticed as a bricklayer in London where he worked on the new station at King's Cross. He became a bare-knuckle fighter, appearing at clandestine and brutal contests which had few rules or time inhibitions, and which ended only when one fighter could go on no longer. His serious career began in 1849 and in 1853 he made his first attempt to be heavyweight champion of England when he met Nat Langham in a match lasting 61 rounds of about 90 seconds each. It was his first and last defeat. He was suc-cessful in his quest to be champion in 1857, defeating William Perry, and was the last holder of the title before the introduction of the Queensberry Rules in 1867.

Sayers was the first English boxer to take part in an international match when he fought the American, John C. Heenan in 1860. This epic match lasted 2 hours 20 minutes and ended in a brawl, an invasion by spectators, the flight of the referee and a draw being called. Sayers is said to have broken his right arm, and Heenan his left hand.

Sayers retired soon afterwards except for exhibition bouts, but aided by a public subscription which raised the enormous sum of £3,000, he bought a house in Camden Town, thought by one authority to be 51 Camden Street, then known as 10 Belle Vue Cottages. Other authorities say that he was accustomed to the area, having been born at what was then 45 Bayham Street, and had been landlord of the Laurel Tree pub on the corner of that street and Greenland Road in 1847.

Sayers' death was either from tuberculosis or diabetes, and he was buried at Highgate Cemetery after a massive funeral procession travelled

167. *Tom Sayers in his carriage, together with his dog Lion.*

168. *The dog Lion sits prominently in the funeral procession of Tom Sayers in 1865, as it leaves Camden Town for Highgate Cemetery. The Britannia at the corner of Parkway and the High Street, is on the right, with the Mother Red Cap to the left.*

from Camden High Street, preceded by his pet mastiff 'Lion'. A large monument was erected there, complete with a statue of the dog. Lion himself was sold off together with Sayers' other effects.

The Second World War

Three areas of Camden Town were badly hit by bombing. **Camden Town Underground Station** and its hinterland was badly damaged on 14 October 1940 – the evidence is still on one wall of the station. The blast also destroyed buildings on the site of what has been used lately by the Buck Street/ Camden Market. Several people were killed in this incident. The Hawley Crescent Board School was also a casualty.

Previously, on 9 September, a high explosive bomb had dropped on the east side of Harrington Square, just south of Mornington Crescent station. Three houses were demolished, and as our illustration shows, a bus was blown into the terrace. The passengers and crew had only just vacated the vehicle to seek the safety of a

trench shelter in the square. Two members of the St Pancras ARP squad received George medals for their bravery in rescuing casualties buried beneath rubble. Eleven people were killed here.

Further to the south around the **Cumberland Basin** a great deal of bombing occurred, destroying many houses, and eventually opening the way for this area to be comprehensively developed. Nearby, the old Ophthalmic Hospital in **Albany Street** was destroyed. Extensive damage occurred on the worst night of the London Blitz, 10/11 May 1941, around the Hampstead Road railway bridge.

Other buildings which were badly damaged during the war were St Paul's church in **Camden Square**, where also nos 12-26 had to be demolished later. The main building of the **North London Collegiate School for Girls** in Sandall

169. *A bus blown against a house in Harrington Square in 1940.*

170. Bomb damage at Camden Town Underground station.

171. Harold Trill's business was established in the 1890s at 131 High Street but later moved to 78 on the other side of the road. It traded there until the mid 1980s.

Road was hit in 1940. St Matthew's School in Arlington Road was destroyed as was the **Congregational Chapel**. There were many casualties in Cliff Road where the newly opened block, Camden House, received a hit. No. 10 Regent's Park Road was bombed and is now replaced by a small block of flats designed by Erno Goldfinger. Nearby, severe damage was caused to **Cecil Sharp House** and, in 1940, to **St Mark's church**.

Before the war began the Council had bought the **Drill Hall** in Camden High Street as an ARP centre, and there was a control room round the corner in Pratt Street. Ration books and gas masks were distributed from the Drill Hall. A shelter was built beneath Camden Town station in two tunnels, 150ft apart, with a capacity for 8000 people. However, this was not completed until late 1942, when conventional bombing had stopped, and it was not used by the public until July-October 1944 when the V1 and V2 missiles were introduced. V1s fell on Rochester Place and Hawley Road.

Shops past and present

Old street directories of Camden Town not only emphasise the workaday nature of Camden Town's shops, but also the number of specialties that have disappeared. At the end of the 1890s the High Street could boast a coal merchant, church decorator, milliner, umbrella maker, bedding maker, invalid and baby carriage maker, glass stainer, parquet manufacturers, a saddler, corn merchant, dairy, bootmaker, oilman, muffin baker, mantle dealer, tripe dresser, lead merchant and harness maker, not to mention numerous cheesemongers. All these old family or one-person businesses were, fortunately, photographed at the beginning of the twentieth century, for when the Northern Line was constructed beneath the High Street it was felt necessary to have very detailed photographs of the premises lining the road either to prove or disprove later claims for subsidence. This invaluable collection of photographs is at the Camden Local Studies and Archives Centre at Holborn Library.

In the 1890s there were only

172. No. 80, Camden High Street, the premises of the local newspaper, the St Pancras Gazette. *One of the many photographs taken in 1904 before the construction of the Northern Line beneath the High Street so as to judge if any subsidence had subsequently damaged the premises.*

173. Pitkin, fishmongers in the High Street. One of the many elaborate displays of goods to be found in butchers', greengrocers' and fishmongers' shops.

★ Marshall Roberts ... can supply your Business Needs

WINDOW TREATMENTS

Whatever the window treatment may be, whether for home or business, you may rest assured that we can supply you with just that treatment most suitable to your particular need. Estimates free and patterns submitted.

* *Curtains, etc., second floor.*

FURNISHING SCHEMES

Whether it be furniture for home or business consult us, and by so doing prove the quality and value our "cash only" policy permits us to give you. Complete schemes prepared and everything done to help you.

* *Furniture, lower ground floor.*

FLOOR COVERINGS

If it be for home or business we definitely say our quality at our prices present the most outstanding value possible. Let us measure and quote for your next job—free, of course.

* *Floorcoverings, second floor.*

174. An advertisement for Marshall Roberts, the large general store in Camden High Street, opposite the Underground station.

two chain stores in the High Street: the tobacconist Salmon & Gluckstein, out of whose families the J. Lyons food empire emerged, was at 181 High Street; and Home & Colonial at 241, as well as in Queen's Crescent, Kentish Town, taking advantage of the street market trade there, just like the young John Sainsbury. Older readers will remember Home & Colonial stores all over London, which at first sold mainly dairy products and then between the wars stocked a more extensive range. Eventually this com-pany, plus another well-known name, Maypole Dairy, together with Pearks and Lipton's, were merged under the umbrella of Allied Suppliers.

By 1911 there was a scatter-ing of familiar names – all on the west side of the road, for by then the best sites on the east side had been taken by **Bow-man Bros.**, a shop which is dealt with separately in this book. We find the London Penny Bazaar Co. at 133. This was a small chain that had cop-ied the methods of Michael Marks who had already estab-lished Marks & Spencer shops elsewhere. Marks had begun in Leeds, selling goods from a stall. His policy was to have a fixed price – no haggling – and the public was at liberty to han-dle the goods before purchase. M & S bought up the London Penny Bazaar chain in 1913. There was a Lipton's tea and provisions at 161, and a True Form Boot Co. at 169. Wool-worth's did not appear until the 1930s.

An important business was at no. 80 High Street. Here R & J Widdicombe published the *St Pancras Gazette* from 1866; un-fortunately for posterity and historians one of the Widdicombes was a St Pancras councillor for the Municipal Reform party (Conservatives) and the newspaper reports of council business of the time are therefore quite partial. Also local councillors were Harold Trill and his son, who sold sta-tionery and typewriters, a busi-ness established in 1903. Both father and son became mayors of the borough. That business, originally on the west side of the road but latterly at no. 78, closed in the 1980s.

A survival from the 19th cen-tury is jewellers, J A Lake at no. 33. Here since 1872, the premises were restored to their former opulence in the 1990s. In 1920, Frank Romany, who had had a shop in Soho, opened an ironmongery busi-ness at no. 34 – it moved later to 52-6. It was notable in Camden Town for being an early DIY store. The family sold the business in the 1980s, but it still trades.

Virtually every town of note had its large drapery store in an age when people or their servants made their own clothes, when drapes them-selves were common furnish-

175. *Nicholson and Wordley were large drapers in the High Street opposite the Underground station. The site of their store was later taken by Marshall Roberts.*

176. *The jewellers, A Mears & Co, at 73 and 75 High Street, probably c. 1905.*

ings, and when more bed clothes were necessary in poorly heated houses. The usual pattern was for one store to be the most successful and gradually expand along a terrace of shops until the time came to completely rebuild as an emporium. Camden Town had two such establishments, next door to each other, facing what would later be an entrance to Camden Town Underground. In the 1890s nos. 197-203 High Street were occupied by Nicholson & Wordley, established by about 1841, and nos. 205-209 by W W Broadhead (1871). By 1910 Marshall Roberts had bought up Nicholson & Wordley with Broadhead's out of business, and then took over the remainder of the frontage. The site was then redeveloped as a single store; this was replaced after the last war by the London Co-op – the structure is still there but is now used by a number of shops selling the sort of merchandise associated with Camden markets.

Montagu Saxby, selling trunks, suitcases and portmanteaux, was once a familiar sight at 24 Camden Road, having taken over a business established early in the 20th century by Frank Leader; it then moved to 8 Kentish Town Road, but its shop is now empty.

T B Westacott, house agents and auctioneers, were long established until recent times at 74 Camden Road. One Westacott was a St Pancras borough councillor and in the debates as to whether the borough should build a public library he commented: "Books of reference can be seen free at the British Museum by all who care to take the trouble", and implied that those who read works of fiction should not be encouraged to do so by the council.

At 46 Camden Road, until recently, was W. Johnson, opticians, who had been there since 1902. This was a branch of the firm's main premises in Tottenham Court Road, near Maple's – the company could boast that it was one of the oldest opticians in London. The main shop closed in the 1990s.

The street directory entries for Parkway (then Park Street) for the 1890s indicate a higher class of shop than the High Street, including a cigar maker and a number of upholsterers, together with a Female Servants' Registry Office. William Heal, at no. 92, was an ironmonger, but his sons, John and Wilfred, developed the business into a reputable building firm that stayed in Parkway until the 1990s.

Parkway in the 1980s and '90s was on its way to becoming a boutique street, benefiting from the stream of people to Camden markets. At the time of writing (June 2007) there is much renovation and change going on. The Regent Bookshop at no. 73 closed in the face of overwhelming competition from Waterstone in the High Street, The graphic supplies firm of Robertson & Co, went in the 1980s, the old Henley's car showroom at the Regent's Park end has been empty for some time, the Camden Stores pub, ineptly renamed the Rat & Parrot, is being renovated and converted, but outside opening hours the Odeon cinema is looking very sad on the exterior, as though it isn't in business at all.

The many small shops of Chalk Farm have changed entirely as well. What used to be 'useful' shops catering for working-class families, have given way to restaurants, bars and boutiques for a quite different local population. These old businesses are fondly recalled in *Primrose Hill Remembered* (2001) and Caroline Cooper's *A History of the shops in Primrose Hill* (2006).

Walter Sickert

The painter Walter Sickert (1860-1942) had many connections with Camden Town and with Camden in general. His family, of Danish descent, moved to England in 1868, and Sickert was a student at University College School until he was expelled. His early ambition was to be an actor, and he played in Edward Irving's company. In 1881 came a change of direction when he became a pupil at the Slade and soon became a protégé of Whistler, whose studio was in Chelsea.

In 1885 Sickert married Ellen Cobden, the daughter of the free trade politician, the late Richard Cobden. It was not an easy marriage and they divorced in 1899 though, ironically, in 1905 he took rooms at 6 Mornington Crescent where he overlooked the Cobden statue at the southern end of the High Street. During his marriage he had a studio in Robert Street, off Hampstead Road and in this period did many of his depictions of

the old Bedford Music Hall. He became associated with the newly-established New English Art Club, which sought to counterbalance with modern work the stagnant taste of the Royal Academy.

Sickert then went abroad for six years, particularly to Dieppe, which he loved. On his return in 1910 he founded the **Camden Town Group**, and also ran an etching class at 208 Hampstead Road, and later a school at no. 140.

He and Spencer Gore shared a studio in Brecknock Road, and he also had studio accommodation in Granby Terrace, just south of Mornington Crescent, where he painted his famous painting, *Ennui*.

After a second marriage to Christine Angus they lived briefly in Harrington Square and between 1912 and 1914 in Gloucester Crescent. In 1917 he had a house in Camden Road, and in 1931 a room at Sylvia Gosse's house, also in Camden Road, and a studio in Whitcher Place, a tiny turning off Rochester Mews.

Spiritualists

Tucked away in Rochester Square is the Spiritualist Centre Temple. Various stones on the exterior of the building relate some of its history. There are two foundation stones, each laid in 1926, one by Ernest Beard and the other by Sir Arthur Conan Doyle. Doyle's fame as the creator of Sherlock Holmes has obscured, in modern times, his obsession with Spiritualism, a cult that began in America in 1848 and was given new life after the First World War when distraught relatives were persuaded that they could communicate with dead loved ones.

177. The Spiritualist church in Rochester Square, 2007.

Doyle, then an unsuccessful physician practising in the backwater of Southsea, became interested in Spiritualism early in the 1880s. In 1893 he joined the British Society for Psychical Research, whose members included the future Prime Minister Arthur Balfour and the scientist and Camden Town resident, **Oliver Lodge**. The Sherlock Holmes stories began in 1887 and provided a vital income as his medical career deteriorated. He publicly announced his belief in Spiritualism in 1916 and was to vigorously assert its beliefs until his death in 1930. In 1920 he was derided for his belief in fairies as a result of his conviction that some photographs taken in Cottingley, by two young sisters, purported to show fairies. One of the sisters admitted as late as 1983 that they were fakes. In 1926, the same year as he laid the foundation stone in Rochester Square, he published his *History of Spiritualism*.

Another stone on the wall of the building commemorates the journalist Hannen Swaffer (1879-1962), who wrote for all the main tabloids of the day.

Steam Power

The old Ophthalmic Hospital in **Albany Street** was later the base for two ventures experimenting with the use of steam power.

The first was pioneered by an American, Jacob Perkins (b. 1766), who, having settled in London, joined with two other entrepreneurs to print banknotes. Their company also printed the first postage stamp – the Penny Black. But Perkins was primarily interested in the growing use of steam to perform industrial tasks. He was particularly involved with a 'steam gun', which he developed in Albany Street as from 1824. In December 1825 a demonstration of this invention was held there. *The Times* reported:

"Soon after 8 o'clock [am] patroles [*sic*] were observed stationed on all the roads leading towards the manufactory, accompanied by men with placards on boards, warning

179. *Goldsworthy Gurney, 1823, a lithograph by W Sharp after S C Smith.*

all passengers on horseback or in carriages to go through the Regent's Park, instead of proceeding by the high road leading in front of the manufactory. Since a fatal accident, which occurred several months ago, where a lady threw herself from a gig in consequence, as it was at the time incorrectly supposed, of her horse having taken fright at the prodigious noise made by the steam gun ..."

Those attending the demonstration included the Marquis of Salisbury, the Master General of the Ordnance, the Duke of Wellington and a committee of Engineer and Artillery officers. The gun comprised a "succession of tubes filled with [musket] balls, fixed in a wheel and falling by their own gravity into the barrel." Perkins claimed that it could fire 1000 balls a minute.

One paper predicted that if the gun were used then wars would be very short since it could kill so many men so quickly. The gun was not used in a war, probably because of the difficulty of managing such steam power in battle.

Perkins left Albany Street in 1926 and the building was then occupied by Goldsworthy Gurney (1793-1875), whose experiments were directed at the use of steam in road transport. The science of management of high-pressure steam was then in its

178. *Goldsworthy Gurney's Steam Carriage on its route to Bath.*

180. *St Augustine's Road, c.1904.*

infancy and his experiments were hazardous. In 1827 he was able to announce in *The Times* that he had recently run steam carriages around Regent's Park. The main doubt was the carriage's ability to go up hills, and Gurney therefore demonstrated its ability up Highgate West Hill, a gradient of 1-in-9. Gurney wrote:

"We left the manufactory in Albany-street at half past four a.m. and reached the foot of the hill in 14 minutes. The carriage began to ascend the hill at the rate of about three miles per hour, and increased its rate as it proceeded up the hill to between four and five ... On surmounting the hill, I stopped with the intention of returning; but a number of persons who had observed the manner in which the carriage went up the hill, cheered us, and induced me to take the carriage through Highgate town, on the Finchley road, at the rate of 15 miles an hour..." On the reverse journey one of the wheels collapsed but no one was hurt.

The most significant journey was one from London to Bath and back in July 1829. The vehicle attracted the violent opposition of unemployed weavers at Melksham who felt that in some way his invention would harm their chances of finding work. Despite his many successes and some commercial investment, Gurney's efforts ended in failure and he closed the Albany Street works in 1831, two years after Shillibeer introduced his popular horse-drawn omnibus along the New Road. (*See* David Hayes 'The Regent's Park Manufactory and two steam pioneers' in *Camden History Review* 30, 2006).

Street name origins

The Camden family accounts for a large number of street names in Camden Town. Their land on the east side of the High Street, in *Cantelowes* manor, was once a *Prebend* of St Paul's Cathedral. In 1790, just before development there began, the prebendary was the Rev. Tho-

mas *Randolph. St Augustine* was reputed to be the founder of Old St Pancras church. An early farmer of the area was John Jeffreys (1670) whose descendant, Elizabeth *Jeffreys* of *Brecknock* Priory, married the then unknown barrister, Charles *Pratt*. As was the custom, the property then passed to him. Pratt was later made Viscount *Bayham* and eventually Earl Camden. His son, John, was created *Marquis* Camden, who had two daughters, *Georgiana* and *Caroline*, and a son, George, who married Harriet *Murray*, daughter of the bishop of *Rochester*. The builder of much of the early development of Camden Town was Augustine *Greenland*.

The Southampton family lent their names to streets on the west side of the High Street. A prominent Royalist during the Civil Wars of the 17th century was Sir Henry Bennet, who was made Earl *Arlington* on the Restoration and awarded the manor of Tottenhall. His daughter, then aged 5, was married to Charles II's illegiti-

181. *Plender Street c.1905, when it was known as King Street.*

182. *Rochester Road, c.1907. Remarkably, this postcard was sent from no. 22 to an address in Brazil in 1907 and has since found its way back to England.*

mate son, Henry *Fitzroy*. A family friend was Richard Wellesley, Earl of *Mornington*.

A 40-acre estate had been held by Dr James *Hawley*. His son, Sir Henry Hawley, began to develop it in partnership with Lewis *Buck* of Hartland Abbey. A descendant, was George *Stucley* Buck.

Crowndale, Harrington, Hurdwick, Ampthill, Oakley, Lidlington and *Goldington* are all derived from the Duke of Bedford's various estates.

In Chalk Farm, Rothwell Street is named after the Marquess de *Rothwell* who lived in **Regent's Park Road**, and Sharpleshall Street, built by him, is named for his home, Sharples Hall, in Lancashire.

Lesser-known individuals remembered are Sydney *Baynes*, the chief electrical engineer for St Pancras Council and William *Plender*, an eminent chartered accountant who worked for a number of important bodies, including the Metropolitan Water Board; the street was originally King Street and was changed in 1937. *Beatty* Street, (also named in 1937), off Arlington Road, commemorates Nelson's surgeon, Sir William *Beatty* – it was originally called Nelson Street. Prowse Place is named from Captain Sir William *Prowse*, one of Nelson's captains. He lived for some years in the Euston Road. Nearby Miller Street indicates John *Miller*, a local builder. James *Delancey* of Marylebone was granted land by the Fitzroy family in Camden Town in 1795. It is possible that he also gave his name to James Street (now *Jamestown* Road).

Near the Regent's Canal where it goes beneath Camden Road are *Lyme* Street and *Rousden* Street, both of them Dorset names, and no doubt to do with the origins of a builder. *Cliff* Road and Villas were once Clifton, and probably celebrated the completion of Brunel's famous bridge at Clifton. Their name was shortened in 1937.

Other street names are dealt with in separate entries.

Theatro Technis

At 26 Crowndale Road is the Greek Theatro Technis, in the building which was formerly the **Old St Pancras Church House**, as can be seen by the inscription outside. This theatre stems from the Greek Arts Theatre Club, founded in 1957 by George Eugeniou to serve the growing Greek Cypriot community. At first they were housed in an old garage in Camden Mews, and then after seven years in a disused railway shed on the Maiden Lane depot south of Agar Grove. Theatro Technis moved to their present building in 1978.

Productions are of an international flavour. There is also a photographic dark room which can be used, and the organization runs an advice group for minority groups.

Tottenhall Manor

The ancient manor of Tottenhall in the parish of St Pancras was generally to the west of the line now represented by Tottenham Court Road, Hampstead Road, Camden High Street, Kentish Town Road and Highgate Road up to, and possibly including, Kenwood. The area of Chalk Farm was in the small manor of Rugmere, but there is some evidence that this was a sub-manor of Tottenhall. Tottenhall manor house stood on the east side of Hampstead Road, between Tolmers Square and Euston Road.

The manor was owned, as **Cantelowes** was, by prebendaries of St Paul's Cathedral until the Reformation, at which point the Crown possessed it. The lease was granted by Charles II in 1668 to his close friend Henry Bennet, Earl of Arlington. Bennet's daughter, Isabella, married Henry Fitzroy, the illegitimate son of the king and Barbara Villiers. A grandson of this marriage, Charles Fitzroy, was able in 1768 to purchase the valuable freehold of Tottenhall at a bargain price – the Act of Parliament to enable this was passed at a time when his brother, the 3rd Duke of Grafton, was prime minister. To complete his riches, Charles was created Baron Southampton in 1780, by which time he was already issuing building leases on the west side of Camden High Street.

H G Wells

As a student, Herbert George Wells (1866-1946) lodged at 181 Euston Road, existing on a maintenance grant of 1 guinea per week, which had to pay for rent, clothes, fares and food. From 1888 to 1891 he stayed with his aunt and cousin Isabel at 46 Fitzroy Road – Isabel became his first wife in 1891. Probably, his residence here led to him using Primrose Hill as the landing place for Martians in his *War of the Worlds*, published in 1896. In 1889 he obtained a junior teaching job at the Henley House School in West Hampstead – one of his pupils there was Alan (later A.A.) Milne, the son of the school's proprietor. Armed with a degree in Zoology, Wells took on another and better paid job at a

183. H. G. Wells.

184. Henry Willis.

crammer called University Correspondence College. It was here that he met a pupil, Catherine Robbins, who was later to be his mistress and then his second wife.

They rented a room at 7 Mornington Place in 1894. Their landlady evicted them when she discovered they were not yet married and they moved around the corner to no. 12 Mornington Terrace. Here, they stayed from 1894 until 1898, living, according to Wells, "in sin and social rebellion". At this address he wrote *The Time Machine*, *The Island of Dr Moreau* and *The Wonderful Visit*.

Henry Willis

'Father' Henry Willis (1821-1901) was the most famous organ builder of his day, and his instruments are still used in places of worship and major buildings throughout the country and abroad. He made the giant organ used at the Great Exhibition in 1851 and was subsequently asked to build the organ for the Royal Albert Hall. Other major installations are at Westminster Abbey, Gloucester, Salisbury, Wells, Lincoln, Durham,

Canterbury and Winchester Cathedrals, Blenheim Palace, Alexandra Palace and the Royal Academy of Music. His organ at Windsor Castle was destroyed by the fire there in 1992.

His factory, called the Rotunda, was sandwiched between a school at the Kentish Town end of Royal College Street and Rochester Place.

The Rotunda was originally built in 1824 by George Lever to display panoramic sketches of London composed by Thomas Hornor (1785-1844), who had accomplished them while suspended on a platform of the scaffolding above the dome of St Paul's Cathedral while the ball and cross were being replaced. (He began work at three o'clock in the morning, climbing 616 stairs and four *external* ladders.) Panoramas became popular and the building was taken over by another practitioner, Robert Burford (1791-1861), who exhibited his own works in Leicester Square and the Diorama in Regent's Park. He also employed Camden Town resident, Henry Courtney Selous, (*see* **Anti-Apartheid Movement**) to paint at least 35 panoramas for him

(Selous kept a diary of life in the painting room 1833-4). The panoramic views could be 40 feet high and 80 feet long.

In 1865 the building was taken by Willis and his firm until 1905. Then the Rotunda was demolished and the school was extended over the site. Of late it was occupied by, St Richard of Chichester School, but it has now been converted into apartments.

The Workhouse

The first St Pancras workhouse was opened in 1731 in St Pancras Way, about where Agar Grove now joins. It is not certain which side of the road it was on. Ratepayers throughout the next 150 years persistently rationed the amount of aid that could be given to indigent and unemployed parishioners for good reason or none. Workhouses were meant to be unpleasant, to deter too long a stay in them. The St Pancras building was declared unsafe in 1772, but it was not until 1775 that parish officials met to consider the adaptation of a "house called Mother Black Caps, or the Half Way House". This was on the site of today's Camden Town Underground station. But it was yet another three years before inmates were installed.

In 1787 it was noted that the wards were so overcrowded at the new place that five or six persons slept to a bed, and there was a great risk of fever. Rooms were small, inadequately ventilated and the timbers were decayed. The Vestry minutes record in 1809 that "On examining the bedsteads, the number is 224, 52 of which are single and 97 double bedsteads, all of which may be fit

185. *The second St Pancras Workhouse, as depicted on King's Panorama. It moved here in 1778 to the former premises of the Mother Black Cap, the location of today's Camden Town Underground station. The site also included stocks and a pound for stray animals.*

for use if they be cleansed from vermin." The remaining 75 were regarded as useless.

The placing of the workhouse on this site underlined the undesirability and isolation of the area. As Frederick Miller, a 19th-century historian of St Pancras noted, it was possible then, with the aid of a telescope, to check the time of day by pointing it at the clock on the tower of St Mary's church, Islington. **King's Panorama** (above) shows the building *c.*1800, with stocks and a pound for stray animals outside. Indeed, much earlier than this the site had been proposed as one on which to erect some gallows.

The poor, especially workhouse inhabitants, leave few historical footprints, but by good fortune, a recent book *(see below)* has touched on the life of one of the inmates of this workhouse. Robert Blincoe, born *c.*1792 somewhere in St Pancras, presumed illegitimate, was left in the Camden Town workhouse four years later. At the age of seven he was apprenticed to mill owners in Nottinghamshire and was obliged to work 14 years in an industry that relied on tied and sweated labour. And yet, heroically, Blincoe was talented enough to rise above such a start in life. He began his own mill and at the same time campaigned for a reduction of hours for child workers. He saved enough to give his own children a good education – one of them went to Cambridge University and later became a clergyman at St Luke's, Old Street.

It could have turned out very differently. In his memoirs, Blincoe recalled the emotional emptiness of his time in the workhouse as a young boy. He spent hours gazing out from its upper windows, making plans to escape. His mother died soon after his arrival in the workhouse and parish authorities subsequently refused to tell him her name. Most distressing to him were those occasions when other workhouse children received visits from family and friends, though he had no visitors at all. (*See* John Waller, *The real Oliver Twist: Robert Blincoe, a life that illuminates an age* (2005), *or see* the same author 'The humblest beginnings: Robert Blincoe's St Pancras years' in *Camden History Review* 30 (2006).

The Working Men's College

The Industrial Revolution had as its cultural counterbalance in the 1820s and 1830s, the formation of educational establishments and associations for both middle and working classes. Middle-class Literary & Scientific Institutes and Mechanics' Institutes were in most towns and cities, and in 1826 the Society for the Diffusion of Useful Knowledge was formed with the aim of spreading education to all classes. Political unrest at the inequality of Society inspired the Chartist Movement of the 1840s. Many issues were argued – the long working hours of the poorer classes, the separation of Church and State, the iniquities of the Poor Law, and into this melée of causes came Temperance, Secularism and the want of educational facilities. At about this time the Christian Socialist movement emerged, led by Frederick Denison Maurice, Thomas Hughes and Charles Kingsley, and soon a coterie of influential people took an active interest. Their chief tenet was co-operation. Maurice spelt it out:

186. *The Common room at the Working Men's College c.1904.*

"The watchword of the Socialist is co-operation – the watchword of the Anti-Socialist is competition…"

To this belief they added their Christian beliefs and Maurice even declared that "Christian Socialism is in my mind the assertion of God's order."

They were not revolutionaries, but favoured gradualism by continual reform, just as the Fabian Society (1884) was to do.

Their earliest social work, in 1848, was an elementary evening school in Holborn, teaching the 3Rs to impoverished and illiterate students. By 1853 the principal leaders were giving talks and evening classes in a hall in Eastcastle Street, off Oxford Street. It was from these that the Working Men's College developed. It opened with an inaugural address by Maurice on 30 October, 1854 at 31 Red Lion Square in Holborn. The College later moved to Great Ormond Street and then, in 1904, the Prince of Wales laid the foundation for the present building in Crowndale Road. Designed by W D Caröe, it included 30 classrooms, laboratories and a gymnasium. An extra floor was added in the 1930s. The first students were admitted in October 1905, the same year that saw the formation of the Workers' Educational Association.

The general admission of women is comparatively recent. This was still being discussed by the College's Council in 1951. Then a brief speech was made from the back of the room: "Mr Chairman, I think we ought to have women, but I move that we don't." This was adopted by a large majority.

At the time of writing (April 2007) the college is appealing for money for much-needed modernization of the building. Around 75% of the students are on benefits, and a third of the courses are provided free.

York and Albany

For many years the York and Albany pub (named after the Prince Regent's brother) at the Regent's Park end of Parkway has been empty. Owned by the Crown Estate, it was destined for substantial interior development, together with an extension to the rear. However, it is a John Nash building thought to be his only public house, and the Camden Civic Society, and in particular Marion Kamlish, have fought persistently against some of the modernization plans.

The building now has a new owner and, at the time of writing (June 2007), renovation and refurbishment is well in hand, to the general satisfac-

187. *Detail from Illustration 134, showing the York & Albany as built by Nash, with a colonnade at side and front. This space was later filled in for an extension to the front bar.*

tion of the Civic Society. It seemed likely that the building, to be primarily a hotel, restaurant and bar, would be rechristened 'Magnolia', but the present owner has now promised it will retain its old name.

A drawing by Thomas Shepherd in 1829 *(ill. 187)* shows that it had a pillared colonnade on the front and side elevations.

Zoological Gardens

The Zoological Society of London was founded in 1826 with the intention of forming a collection of species that would be the basis for scientific research and public interest. The Society was able to lease a site from the Crown Commissioners in the north-east of Regent's Park which was bisected by the Outer Circle and included a stretch of the Regent's Canal. Originally, also, the Society wished to include a Botanical Garden and a Museum.

The project was suggested by Sir Stamford Raffles who had made his career in the colonial service, particularly in the Far East where, in 1819 he founded Singapore – the luxury Raffles hotel there recalls his name. Unlike many colonial administrators, he is recalled with some admiration for his attempts to eliminate the slave trade and reduce opium dealing, as well as setting up civic administration.

Raffles (1781-1826) was the first President of the Society, but he died of a brain tumour in 1826, two years before the Zoo was opened. He had retired to Hendon and was entitled to be buried at his parish church, St Mary's. However, the vicar of Hendon, whose family fortune was based on the slave trade, refused to have Raffles buried within the church for his opposition to slaving. Instead the body was interred outside the building but, in 1915, it was re-interred inside the extended church.

The Zoo opened to members in 1828 with buildings designed by Decimus Burton – the architect of the mansion called The Holme overlooking the lake in the Park. The general public was admitted in 1847. At the beginning, the Society had 194 species and varieties (a total of 627 animals); today it has 651 species. The Society was early on presented with animals from the Royal Menageries at Windsor and the Tower of London, and also some from Mr Cross, who ran a private menagerie at Exeter Change in the Strand.

An Indian elephant came from the Royal collection, and in 1835 came the first chimpanzee, followed by four giraffes a year later. A hippopotamus arrived in 1850 and an orangutan in 1851. The world's first reptile house opened here in 1843, and an aquarium ten years later. An insect house was introduced in 1881. The first giant panda did not arrive until 1938.

There had long been misgivings at the accommodation for the animals. Burton's buildings were, for the most part, villas or follies, designed more for their looks than their suitability for the inmates. In particular the lion house was criticized. One magazine in 1869 complained that: "We are all tired of the dismal menagerie cages. The cramped walk, the weary restless movement of the head ... the bored look, the artificial habits ... Thousands upon thousands will be gratified to learn that a method of displaying lions and tigers, in what may be called by comparison, a state of nature, is seriously contemplated at last." This heralded Salvin's new lion and tiger house, erected in 1876, and which many older readers will remember also as quite inadequate.

The Mappin Terraces for bears and goats, designed by Belcher and Joass, were built in 1913-14 (and were much criticized as being unsuitable), and the famous penguin pool, created by Lubetkin and Tecton, opened in 1934. A bomb dropped on the zebra house during the war and the animals galloped off, one in the direction of Camden Town pursued by keepers.

After the last war there was a spurt of new building, which included the Elephant and Rhino Pavilion (1965), designed by Casson, Conder & Partners, the Aviary ((1964) by Lord Snowdon, and new lion terraces (1976) by J W Toovey. Despite these improvements there were still many voices raised at the restrictive housing of many creatures, particularly the larger animals and the chimps and gorillas.

The Society went through a difficult financial period during the 1980s and was troubled by well-publicised internal feuds. There were also many people who thought that the imprisonment of animals merely for the amusement of the public was now unnecessary given that they were shown to great effect on television and, indeed, in safari parks.

The Society weathered this period and the drop in attendances has been reversed. In April 2007 the Gorilla Kingdom was opened to an enthusiastic public.

Further Reading

Aston, Mark, *The Cinemas of Camden* (1997) (London Borough of Camden).

Bordass, M E E, *Primrose Hill Studios, 1877-83*, unpub. (1981?) (copy at Camden Local Studies & Archives).

Burchell, Doris, *Miss Buss' Second School* (1971).

Camden History Society, *Camden History Review* (published annually)

Camden History Society, *Streets of Camden Town*, ed. Steven Denford and F Peter Woodford (2003).

Camden History Society, *Streets of Kentish Town*, ed. Steven Denford and David A Hayes (2005).

Camden History Society, *From Primrose Hill to Euston Road*, (rev. edition), ed. F Peter Woodford (1995).

Cline, Roger, *Regent's Park and Primrose Hill*, unpub. dissertation (1991).

Colloms, Marianne and Weindling, Dick, *Camden Town and Kentish Town* (2003).

Cooper, Caroline, *A History of the Shops in Primrose Hill since the first ones opened in 1855* (2006).

Cotchin, Prof. Ernest, *The Royal Veterinary College London* (1991).

Country Life, *Old Euston* (1938).

Denford, Steven L J, *Agar Town: The Life & Death of a Victorian "Slum"* (Camden History Society (1995).

Flood, Aidan, *The Irish in Camden* (1991).

Friends of Chalk Farm Library, *Primrose Hill Remembered*, by Residents Past and Present (2001).

Harrison, Gerry, *The Scattering: A History of the London Irish Centre, 1954-2004* (2004).

Hassiotis, Anna, The Greek Cypriot Community in Camden (1991).

Lawrence, Helen, *Music, Art and Politics: a history of the St Pancras & Camden Festivals 1954-1987.* (Camden History Society 2004).

London County Council, *Survey of London, Vol. XIX, St Pancras pt II* (1938).

London Topographical Society, *The Kentish Town Panorama* (facsimile reproduction 1986), drawings by James King, commentary by John Richardson. In association with the London Borough of Camden.

Miller, Frederick, *St Pancras Past and Present* (1874).

Mitchell, P. Chalmers, *Centenary History of the Zoological Society of London* (1929).

Morrell, Rev. R. Conyers, *The Story of Agar Town* (nd).

Napley, Sir David, *The Camden Town Murder* (1987).

Nelson, Sarah, *The History of the Camden Goods Yard*, unpub. article 1986 (copy at Camden Local Studies & Archives).

Newbery, Charles Allen (annotated by Robin Woolven, ed. F Peter Woodford), *Wartime St Pancras, A London borough defends itself* (2006).

Richardson, John, *Camden Town and Primrose Hill Past* (1991).

Richardson, John, *A History of Camden: Hampstead, Holborn and St Pancras* (1999).

Schiele, Jinny, *Post-war Theatre in Camden: a Study of three theatre enterprises (The Bedford, Open Space and Roundhouse 1949-83)*, unpub. thesis (1987), Polytechnic of North London.

Scott Rogers, Jean, *A Short History of St Mark's Church* (1978).

Sheridan, Michael, *Rowton Houses 1892-1954* (1956).

Tindall, Gillian, *The Fields Beneath* (1977).

Waller, John, *The Real Oliver Twist: Robert Blincoe, a Life that illuminates an age* (2005).

Watson, Nigel, *And their works do follow them: The story of North London Collegiate School 1850-2000* (2000).

Whitehead, Jack, *The Growth of Camden Town: AD1800-2000* (1999)

Index